The SMART Programme

<u>S</u>tress <u>M</u>anagement <u>A</u>nd <u>R</u>eduction for <u>T</u>eachers

A Self-Help Guide Using Cognitive Behavioural Techniques

Dr Paulette C. Ogun

Grosvenor House
Publishing Limited

All rights reserved
Copyright © Dr Paulette C. Ogun, 2014

The right of Dr Paulette C. Ogun to be identified as the author of this
work has been asserted by her in accordance with Section 78
of the Copyright, Designs and Patents Act 1988

The book cover picture is copyrighted to Dr Paulette C. Ogun

This book is published by
Grosvenor House Publishing Ltd
28-30 High Street, Guildford, Surrey, GU1 3EL.
www.grosvenorhousepublishing.co.uk

This book is sold subject to the conditions that it shall not, by way of
trade or otherwise, be lent, resold, hired out or otherwise circulated
without the author's or publisher's prior consent in any form of binding
or cover other than that in which it is published and
without a similar condition including this condition being imposed
on the subsequent purchaser.

A CIP record for this book
is available from the British Library

ISBN 978-1-78148-676-4

Important Note

This book is not intended as a substitute for medical advice
or treatment. Any person with a condition requiring
medical attention should consult a qualified
medical practitioner or suitable therapist.

The SMART Programme

<u>S</u>tress <u>M</u>anagement <u>A</u>nd <u>R</u>eduction for <u>T</u>eachers

A Self-Help Guide Using Cognitive Behavioural Techniques

Because Every Teacher Matters

Teaching is a stressful profession! An increasing number of teachers are succumbing to stress related disorders, such as depression and anxiety and/or stress related physical ill-health.

This book sets out the **SMART** (<u>S</u>tress <u>M</u>anagement <u>A</u>nd <u>R</u>eduction for <u>T</u>eachers) **Programme**. It gives teachers tools to combat stress, using a Cognitive Behavioural Therapy (CBT) approach. CBT is a very effective, research validated approach, especially for issues like stress.

The SMART Programme gives clear, practical strategies and advice, including effective psychological techniques. It consists of easy to follow information, questionnaires, worksheets and exercises. The reader is given guidance on how to:

- Identify their personal stressors and signs of stress.
- Change their negative stressful thoughts into more positive enabling ones.
- Carry out a variety of relaxation techniques for mental, emotional and physical relaxation.

Dr Paulette C. Ogun is a practising Chartered Educational Psychologist, who has been advising and supporting teachers for over 10 years. Before this she taught in UK schools for several years. This has given her a rich understanding of the stress experienced by teachers and motivated her to create the SMART Programme.

Contents

List of Figures	xi
Acknowledgements	xiii
About the Author	xv
Part One – Background information	**1**
Chapter One Introduction – Every Teacher Matters	3
Chapter Two Teaching – A High Stress profession	4
Reasons for Teacher Stress	4
Effects of Teacher Stress	4
Chapter Three Dealing With Teacher Stress – What Has Been Done So Far	6
Chapter Four **Why Use CBT?**	8
What Is CBT?	8
The Effectiveness of CBT	10
Part Two – The SMART Programme	**11**
Chapter Five **The Structure of the SMART Programme**	13
Definitions of Stress Used By the SMART Programme	13
Chapter Six **Introduction to Session 1**	15
SMART Programme – Session 1 – Overview	16
What is Stress?	17
A CBT Model of Stress	17
Recognising Your Stress Responses	18
Coping With Work Stress Questionnaire	20
Relaxation Exercise – for a Quick Release of Tension	21
Homework from Session 1	22
Chapter Seven **Introduction to Session 2**	23
SMART Programme – Session 2 – Overview	24
The 15 Thinking Errors – Self Audit	25

Contents

Stress-Inducing Beliefs Indicator	28
Challenging Your Stress-Inducing Thoughts	30
The ABCDE Model of Stress by Dr Albert Ellis	30
Challenging the 15 Thinking Errors	31
Helpful Challenging Questions	37
How to Use the Helpful Challenging Questions to Complete the ABCDEF Challenging Stress-Inducing Thoughts Worksheet	38
Instructions for the Completion of the ABCDEF Challenging Stress-Inducing Thoughts Worksheet	38
A Completed Example of the ABCDEF Challenging Stress-Inducing Thoughts Worksheet	39
The ABCDEF Challenging Stress-Inducing Thoughts Worksheet	40
Meditation Exercise – Letting Go of Thoughts	42
Homework from Session 2	44

Chapter Eight **Introduction to Session 3** 45

SMART Programme – Session 3 – Overview	46
Stress Thought Record	47
Completing a Stress Thought Record to Combat Stress	48
Managing Anger	51
Case Study: Angry Peter	52
Deactivating Your Anger – Exercise	53
Use of Imagery to Reduce Stress Levels	54
Coping Imagery	54
Self-Motivation Imagery	55
Time Projection Imagery	56
Self-Esteem vs. Self-Acceptance	57
Relaxation Imagery	59
Homework from Session 3	60

Chapter Nine **Introduction to Session 4** 61

SMART Programme – Session 4 – Overview	62
Assessing Type A and Type B Behaviours	63
Social Support for Work Problems	64

Do You Procrastinate?	66
Time Management Tips	67
Being Assertive	67
Being Assertive – What Behaviour Do You Tend To Exhibit?	68
Some Assertiveness Techniques	70
Improving Your Physical Health Can Help You Manage and Reduce Your Stress Levels	72
Sample Stress Management Action Plan	75
Stress Management Action Plan	77
Progressive Muscle Group Relaxation	79
Homework from Session 4	80

Part Three – General Information — 81

Footnotes — 83
List of References — 84
Useful Organisations and Websites — 87

List of Figures

4.1 Dysfunctional Cycle　　　　　　　　　　　　　　　　　　　　　　9
4.2 Functional Cycle　　　　　　　　　　　　　　　　　　　　　　　9

Acknowledgements

I would like to thank all the people who have supported and encouraged me in the production of both my doctorate research thesis and this book. Some people I would particularly like to thank are:

- My doctorate tutor, Dr Jeff Matthews for his support and guidance.
- Dr Stephen Palmer from the Centre for Stress Management in London, who has given me permission to use and adapt his materials to create a Programme for teachers.
- My husband Lanre and my daughters, Morayo and Ayanna, for their love and support.
- My sister Steph for her patient proof-reading of my doctorate thesis.
- My daughter Ayanna for her patient proof-reading of this book.
- My parents, Ivy and Samuel Hanson, for their encouragement and prayers.
- My parents' in-law, Elizabeth and Jimi Ogun, for their encouragement and prayers.

About the Author

Dr Paulette C. Ogun has been a practising Chartered Educational Psychologist for over 10 years, in which time she has advised and supported teachers in meeting the needs of children and young people with special educational needs. She is an Associate Fellow of the British Psychological Society and a Senior Associate of the Royal Society of Medicine.

After teaching in UK schools for several years, Dr Ogun started her Educational Psychology career at the Educational Psychology Service in Sunderland in the NE of England. She currently works on a part-time basis for Birmingham Educational Psychology Service in the West Midlands (UK).

Dr Ogun also provides clinical guidance and support to the Mico University College Child Assessment and Research in Education (CARE) Centre in Jamaica, West Indies.

The **SMART** (**S**tress **M**anagement **A**nd **R**eduction for **T**eachers) **Programme** was devised by Dr Ogun as part of her doctoral research. She completed her doctoral degree at the Tavistock and Portman NHS Trust in London, UK (validated by the University of Essex). Her special interest is in promoting the mental health and emotional wellbeing of both adults and children in educational settings.

Part One
Background Information

Chapter One

Introduction – Every Teacher Matters

I have been an Educational Psychologist (EP), advising and supporting teachers in UK schools for over 10 years. Before this I taught in secondary schools in the UK, as well as having other professional roles.

My experience both as a teacher and an EP, going into schools and working closely with teachers, has highlighted how stressful teaching can be on a day-to-day basis. A variety of reasons have been given for teacher stress. Some common ones are heavy workloads; badly behaved children; demanding and/or aggressive parents; and multiple job roles with often overlapping deadlines and demands. This is just the tip of the iceberg!

As an EP, my role is to support children and young people with special educational needs in schools and other educational institutions. This is done directly or indirectly, by working mainly with teachers, as well as with other professionals. I have often thought – "But who is looking after the teachers? They need help too." In the UK, we have had the Government initiative "Every Child Matters". I feel that "Every Teacher Matters" too.

With these thoughts in mind, I carried out a piece of doctoral research using a Cognitive Behavioural Therapy-based approach, utilising strategies which aimed to help a group of teachers manage and reduce their stress levels. The results were powerful! All the teachers who took part in the Programme felt that it had helped them to lower their stress levels and to manage their stress levels better. This was the case whether they had started the Programme with high levels of stress or with mild to normal levels of stress. This positive effect continued well after the Programme had ended – even up to 3 years later (when it was last checked).

In this book, I would like to share with other teachers and educators the strategies which were so effective in helping the teachers I worked with. I have called my Programme the **SMART Programme** – i.e. the **S**tress **M**anagement **A**nd **R**eduction for **T**eachers Programme.

Dr Paulette C. Ogun, C. Psychol, AFBPsS
B.A. (Hons), A.L.C.M., P.G.C.E., A.C.I.S., M.A. (Dist.), MSc. (Dist.), D.Ed.Psych.

Chapter Two

Teaching – A High Stress Profession

Research indicates that teaching is a high stress profession (Kyriacou, 2001; Jepson & Forrest, 2006; Lambert, McCarthy, O'Donnell & Wang, 2009; Klassen, 2010). According to Jepson and Forrest (2006), 41% of teachers report having high stress levels. In addition, Johnson et al. (2005) compared the psychological health of 26 different professions and found teaching to be one of the six most stressful occupations.

Reasons for Teacher Stress

Some common reasons given for teacher stress are time pressures, excessive workloads, maintaining discipline and abusive pupils and parents (e.g. Pithers & Soden, 1998; Austin, Shah & Muncer, 2005). Additional reasons have been given by Brown, Ralph and Brember (2002). These are - poor levels of communication by school managers and hierarchical, distant, management styles; poor perception of teachers by parents who also have unrealistic expectations of what their children can achieve; uncomfortable school environments (e.g. inappropriate classroom sizes with a sense of overcrowding; old and poorly maintained buildings; general lack of cleanliness, particularly in toilets; general lack of environmental resources); and constant change with a link to feelings of powerlessness around this change. Brown et al. (2002) found that the teachers they researched, reported bewilderment and angst at the scope and rate of change and the diversity of roles with which they were having to cope - in particular, at the perceived irrationality behind it all.

Effects of Teacher Stress

Research has indicated that job stress among teachers is associated with mental effects such as low self-efficacy which is a low belief in their abilities (Betoret, 2006); physical effects, such as job related illnesses (McGrath & Huntington, 2007); and reduced or poor job performance (Howard & Johnson, 2004). Research regarding job stress amongst teachers also indicates that prolonged stress can lead to teachers experiencing burnout (Kyriacou, 2001). Burnout is defined as prolonged stress that is characterised by exhaustion (emotional as well as physical) (McCarthy, Lambert, O'Donnell & Melendres, 2009).

The range of physical symptoms associated with teacher stress has been listed in earlier research by Punch and Tuettmann (1990). These include cardiovascular disease, rashes, behavioural changes such as deterioration in relationships and work performance, and psychological reactions, such as confused thinking, anxiety, panic, feeling inadequate and phobias.

Austin et al. (2005) have noted the research finding that more than 40% of teachers have experienced serious symptoms of stress and that the number of referrals of teachers to occupational therapists with stress related disorders such as anxiety, depression and burnout is increasing.

All of this also has a detrimental effect on the learning experience of pupils because of teachers' deteriorated performance, as noted above.

Chapter Three

Dealing With Teacher Stress – What Has Been Done So Far

Researchers have tried to help teachers deal with their stress levels. Bachkirova (2005) has noted that despite all the research and theories into stress and its causes, together with measures being taken to reduce the levels of stress at work, overall statistics show that the problem remains unresolved. She notes that traditional studies correlating self-reported symptoms of stress with a myriad of potential causes cannot produce meaningful results because they do not take into account different perceptions of these, by different individuals at different times (Grimley, 2001). The ability to deal with stress needs to be seen as an individual issue (Kyriacou, 2001). This is especially the case when examining and considering coping strategies to reduce stress (Austin et al., 2005).

The main sources of stress experienced by a particular teacher will be unique to him or her and will depend on the precise complex interaction between their personality, skills, values and circumstances (Kyriacou, 2001). Lending some support to this view are the findings of Roger and Hudson (1995). They looked at stress management training for teachers and found that a key feature in prolonging the experience of stress was a tendency for emotional rumination (i.e. thinking about the situation and emotional upset over and over again), which served to maintain the feelings of tension and upset engendered by the source of stress. They therefore pointed to the need to help individuals develop greater 'emotional control' by terminating such rumination and thereby enabling palliative techniques to be more effective. (Palliative techniques do not deal with the source of stress itself, but are aimed at lessening the feeling of stress that occurs – i.e. in reducing emotional discomfort.) Dewe (1985) concluded that palliative strategies are important as they may enhance an individual's ability to initiate some direct action techniques. The SMART Programme includes palliative techniques.

In his critical review of teacher stress, Jarvis (2002) stated that there is a substantial body of research which has examined the cognitive factors (i.e. factors connected with thinking or conscious mental processes) affecting individual susceptibility to stress amongst teachers. This research has provided a sound base of evidence that cognitive factors underlie individual vulnerability to teacher stress. For example, Chorney (1998) investigated self-defeating beliefs by asking 41 teachers to identify what they must do to be a good teacher. 92% of responses used absolute words, such as 'need', 'must 'etc. Endorsement of these beliefs was widespread in the sample and significantly associated with high levels of stress.

In another study Bibou-Nakou, Stogiannidou and Kiosseoglou (1999) examined the role of attributions (thoughts or views regarding how something has come about). They found a significant association between internal attributions and symptoms of burnout, suggesting that teachers who blame themselves for difficulties are more vulnerable to stress. Similarly, research into self-efficacy (self-belief in one's effectiveness and abilities) as a cognitive vulnerability factor, found that low self-efficacy has a causal relationship with stress symptoms and burnout (e.g. Friedman, 2000; Browers & Tomic, 2000; Skaalvik & Skaalvik, 2007; Schwarzer & Hallum, 2008). All of this is connected to the transactional theory of stress devised by Lazarus and Folkman (1984) which links feelings of stress with a person's perception of their ability to cope with the demands placed on them. If they think they have a problem or feel they cannot cope, then the stress responses may be activated and unpleasant feelings and emotions may be experienced.

Chapter Four

Why Use CBT?

As indicated in the previous chapter, research findings indicate that a teacher's susceptibility to stress and the damaging experience of it, is largely related to their personal cognitions (thoughts and beliefs) about the stressors. This suggests that cognitive interventions designed to improve their cognitions, may reduce the negative effects of stress. Lazarus and Folkman (1984, p. 374) have described Cognitive Behavioural Therapy (CBT) as being "highly compatible" with their Transactional theory of stress. Their theory links feelings of stress with a person's perception of their ability to cope with the demands placed on them. Thus if they feel/think they cannot cope, then they are likely to feel stressed. CBT aims to break such patterns of negative thinking which produce a problem cycle of emotions. Therefore it is an ideal approach to use for the management and reduction of teacher stress. This lends support for its use in the SMART Programme.

What Is CBT?

"CBT is a type of psychotherapy that combines behaviour modification and cognitive therapy. It focuses on cognition (belief), emotion (feeling) and behaviour (action)… [It] highlights how your irrational thoughts (beliefs and assumptions) determine your feelings and affect your choices of your actions and behaviour." (Boyes, 2008, p.10).

Looking at the behavioural aspect of CBT, as noted above, CBT includes encouraging behaviour modification. Working on our behaviours can help us combat feelings of stress. This can include, for example, managing our time better, getting adequate rest and exercising more.

Looking at the cognitive aspect of CBT, this is largely based on the work of Albert Ellis and Aaron Beck in the 1950s, 1960s and 1970s. Both identified that our cognitions can affect the way we feel.

CBT incorporates Ellis's ABC model whereby an activating event (A), triggers certain beliefs (B) which then result in a specific emotional response and consequent behaviour (C).

Beck states that faulty fixed beliefs (or 'schemas') from childhood can also be activated by events which can trigger negative automatic thoughts (Beck & Greenberg, 1974). Consequently these result in negative emotions, behaviours and sometimes bodily reactions (Curwen, Palmer & Ruddell, 2000).

Beck's theory is at the heart of CBT. It states that it is the <u>meaning we attach</u> to a particular situation or event (i.e. our cognitions) that directly causes us problem feelings, not the situation itself (Boyes, 2008). Therefore if we can change our cognitions to non-problematic ones, we can positively change our feelings and reactions/behaviours.

The CBT process aims to move the person from a dysfunctional cycle to a functional cycle.

See figures 4.1 and 4.2 below (adapted from Stallard, 2002, p. 7).

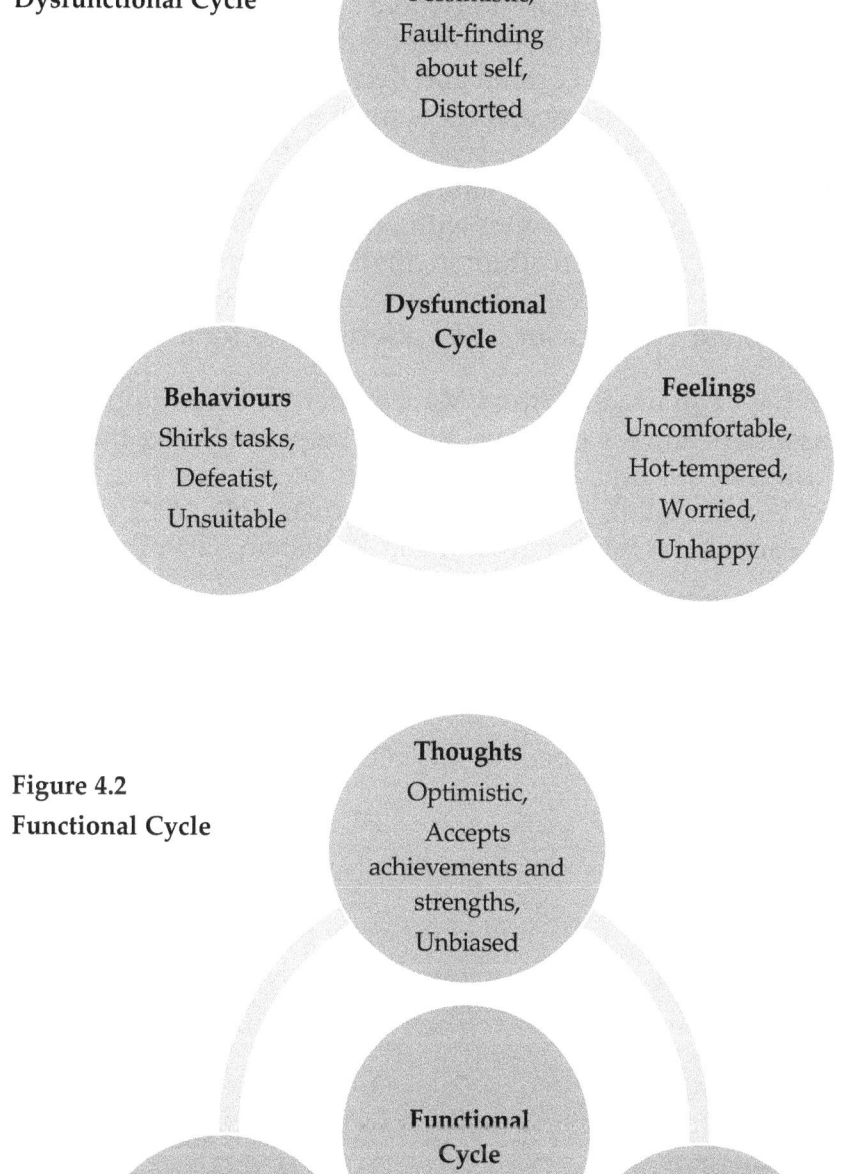

Figure 4.1
Dysfunctional Cycle

Figure 4.2
Functional Cycle

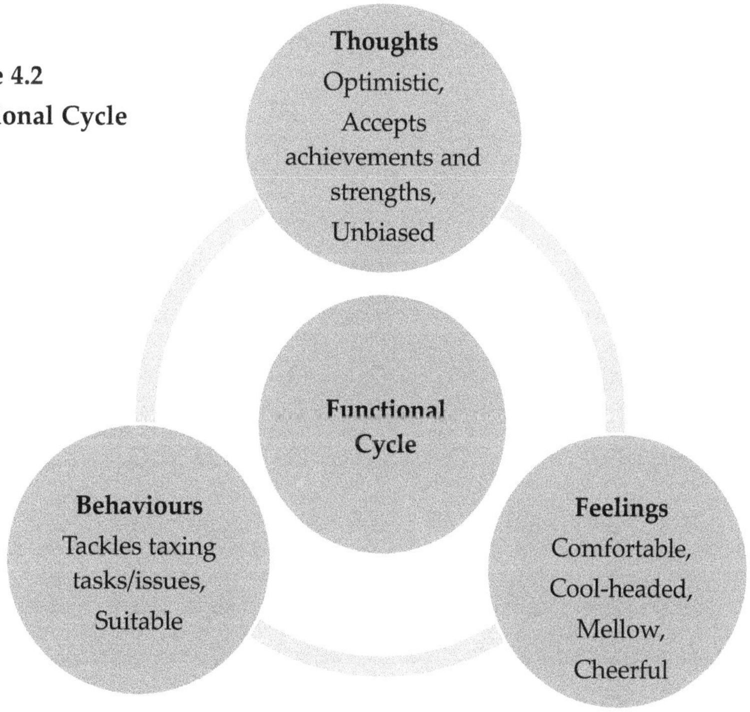

Chapter Four

The Effectiveness of CBT

The SMART Programme, which is based on CBT, is effective because of its use of the CBT approach. There is a strong research base supporting the effectiveness of CBT both in the short-term and longer-term and when compared to other types of treatment, including medication.

For example, in their review of 16 meta-analyses (where several research studies are analysed together to see what they have all found) on treatment outcomes of CBT for a wide range of psychiatric disorders, Butler, Chapman, Forman and Beck, (2006) found support for the efficacy of CBT. CBT was effective in treating many disorders, such as adult and adolescent unipolar depression; generalized anxiety disorder; obsessive compulsive disorder; and post-traumatic stress disorder. Whilst taking into account the limitations of the meta-analytic approach, Butler et al. still found that their findings were consistent with other review methodologies that also provide support for the efficacy of CBT. In addition, there was significant evidence for the long-term effectiveness of CBT for these disorders. The National Institute for Health and Clinical Excellence (2004) has also found evidence for CBT's effectiveness for a variety of conditions.

Where a CBT approach has been used in Stress Management Intervention (SMI) Programmes in the workplace, it has also been very effective. Researchers examining the findings of a number of research studies in this area have found this to be the case (e.g. the meta-analysis of 48 SMI Programmes by van der Klink, Blonk, Schene and van Dijk (2001); and a meta-analysis of 36 SMI Programmes carried out by Richardson and Rothstein, (2008)).

The SMART Programme is an SMI Programme which uses CBT and in this way is similar to those found to be effective by the researchers above. It is designed for teachers to use the strategies in and for their working environment. Hence the effectiveness of the SMART Programme has a solid research base.

Part Two
The SMART Programme

Chapter Five

The Structure of the SMART Programme

First - there is a brief teaching element about stress and its effects on the body. You can carry out an exercise to help you identify your personal stress responses. These cover psychological and emotional responses (e.g. feeling anxious, angry, ashamed, embarrassed); behavioural responses (e.g. aggression, crying, avoidance, increased drinking of alcohol); and physiological responses (e.g. dry mouth, headaches, sweaty palms). Stress responses are closely linked to the negative thoughts, unhelpful core beliefs and dysfunctional assumptions which exacerbate stressful feelings.

Second - you are taught how to identify, challenge and amend your personal negative cognitions (thoughts), so that they become more positive and enabling. This is facilitated by various questionnaires, worksheets and strategies, such as the Stress Thought Record and Coping Imagery.

Third - other cognitive (e.g. Relaxation Imagery) and behavioural (e.g. breathing and muscle relaxation) techniques and exercises are taught to enable you to emotionally and physically relax and reduce your stress levels. Whilst going through the SMART Programme you can set weekly targets and practice techniques learned, for 'homework'. At the end of the Programme you will be able to set long-term goals.

I would encourage you to reward yourself for partial successes as well as complete successes as you go through the Programme, as this is more beneficial to you and will keep you motivated.

The SMART Programme is divided into 4 sessions. Each session can be completed in one go or over several different occasions, according to your needs.

Definitions of Stress Used By the SMART Programme

One definition of occupational stress is – "Stress is the adverse reaction people have to excessive pressures or other types of demand placed on them." (Health and Safety Executive, 2001). The Health and Safety Executive (HSE) has stated that occupational and work-related stress is that which derives specifically from conditions in the workplace (or are exacerbated by such factors) and is thought to arise when workers perceive that they cannot adequately cope with the demands made on them, or with threats to their jobs and the circumstances in which they are carried out.

Kyriacou (2001) has defined teacher stress as the experience of unpleasant negative emotions, such as anger, anxiety, tension, frustration or depression, resulting from some aspect of their work as a teacher. Kyriacou and Sutcliffe (1978) developed a model of teacher stress whereby

Chapter Five

stress is viewed as a negative emotional experience being triggered by the teacher's perception that their work situation constitutes a threat to their self-esteem or well-being.

As author of this book, I agree with all the definitions of occupational and teacher stress set out above. These have been the basis of the main stress definition utilised in this Programme – namely - **"Stress occurs when pressure exceeds your <u>perceived</u> ability to cope."** (Palmer & Cooper, 2007, p.6).

This means that if you feel or believe that you cannot cope, then you will begin to feel stressed. Feeling that you cannot cope involves negative, dysfunctional thoughts and beliefs. The SMART Programme will therefore give the reader the tools to change these types of negative thoughts and beliefs plus provide other cognitive and behavioural stress reducing techniques and exercises, as noted above.

The following sections of this book will set out the SMART Programme's sessions. Each session will be introduced by a summary of what it involves and a table which gives an overview of the contents of that session, in the order in which they should be followed. The tables will also indicate and explain the cognitive and/or behavioural purpose of each activity or technique.

Chapter Six

Introduction to Session 1

This session will enable you to have an understanding of what stress is, by providing a useful definition of stress as used by the SMART Programme. You will also be able to see how stress can be triggered, by examining a CBT Model of Stress. Next we will use a checklist to enable you to identify how you personally respond to stress, so you can be aware of when this is happening from now on and therefore know when to make use of the strategies that the SMART Programme will give you.

We will also take a brief look at the coping strategies you are currently using in your workplace so you can see if there are any gaps which you need to fill. Finally we will end this session with a stress reducing breathing technique.

CHAPTER SIX

SMART Programme – Session 1 – Overview

Name of Technique/Content/Activity	Purpose
What Is Stress? A CBT Model of Stress Is Introduced.	Cognitive: You will learn about stress and its effects. The CBT Model upon which the techniques being taught are based, will also be introduced.
Recognising Your Stress Response – Covering Psychological, Behavioural and Physiological Responses.	Cognitive: You will learn to recognise when you are feeling stressed, so that you can know when you need to use the strategies you will be taught in the Programme.
Your Current Work Stress Coping Strategies.	Cognitive: Helping you think about and identify effective strategies you already use at work which you can build on. Helping you identify gaps which need to be filled.
Quick Release of Tension – Breathing Relaxation Exercise.	Cognitive and Behavioural: A helpful breathing technique which you can use during the following week(s). It incorporates some thinking techniques (i.e. mentally saying "calm in …tension out" as you breathe in and out), as well as some use of imagery.

What is Stress?

- "Stress occurs when pressure exceeds your <u>perceived</u> ability to cope."
  (Palmer & Cooper, 2007, p. 6)

- "The adverse reaction people have to excessive pressures or other types of demand placed on them."
  (Health & Safety Executive, UK, 2001)

A CBT Model of Stress

The ABC Model of Stress

A. Activating event or situation.

B. Beliefs about the event (it is perceived as stressful)

C. Consequences (stress response):

- Emotional e.g. anxiety, anger
- Behavioural e.g. aggression, avoidance
- Physiological e.g. palpitations, sweaty/clammy hands.

(Footnote: 1)

Go through the next few pages and complete the various worksheets.

Chapter Six

Recognising Your Stress Response

Self-Assessment of Your Stress Response
(Tick the ones you have experienced)

Psychological (includes Emotions)

- Angry
- Anxious, apprehensive, frightened
- Ashamed, embarrassed
- Depressed or feeling low
- Guilty
- Jealous
- Mood swings
- Reduced self-esteem or self-worth
- Feeling out of control, helpless
- Suicidal ideas
- Paranoid thinking
- Unable to concentrate
- Intrusive images or thoughts
- Negative images or pictures of situations going wrong
- Images of being out of control
- Images of suicide or death
- Increased daydreaming
- Having a poor self-image
- Nightmares

Behavioural

- Passive behaviour
- Aggressive behaviour
- Irritability, snappiness
- Procrastination
- Increased alcohol consumption
- Increased caffeine consumption (in tea or coffee)
- Comfort eating
- Disturbed sleep patterns (such as waking up early)
- Withdrawing or sulking
- Clenched fists
- Banging a surface (like a table) e.g. with fists
- Compulsive or impulsive behaviour
- 'Checking' rituals
- Poor time management

Self-Assessment of Your Stress Response
(Tick the ones you have experienced)

- Reduced work performance
- Increased absenteeism from work
- Eating/talking/walking fast
- Increased accident-proneness
- Change in interest in sex
- Nervous tics

Physiological/Physical

- Dry mouth
- Clammy hands
- Frequent colds or other infections
- Palpitations or thumping heartbeat
- Breathlessness
- Tightness or pain in the chest
- Feeling faint or fainting
- Migraines
- Vague aches
- Tension headaches
- Backaches
- Indigestion
- Diarrhoea
- Irritable bowel syndrome
- Constipation
- Skin complaints or allergies
- Asthma
- Excess sweating or clammy hands
- Change to the menstrual pattern
- Rapid weight change
- Thrush or cystitis

This exercise will help you to become aware of your responses to stress.

Which symptoms occurred first? In future, use these symptoms as an early-warning sign that you are possibly suffering from stress and may benefit from some action on your part. See your GP if you are experiencing more than 5 of the above symptoms on a regular basis. Some of the more serious symptoms, such as chest pains or suicidal ideas, need more urgent attention.

This list is just a guide. Some of the symptoms you have ticked may reflect a physical problem that needs medical assistance.

(Footnote: 2)

Chapter Six

Coping With Work Stress Questionnaire					
When you have a work-related problem or stress to what extent do you do the following?					
Helpful Behaviour	Never	Rarely	Occasionally	Regularly	Very often
Seek support and advice from managers	1	2	3	4	5
Try to deal with the situation objectively in an unemotional way	1	2	3	4	5
Try to recognise your own limitations	1	2	3	4	5
Talk to understanding colleagues	1	2	3	4	5
Set priorities and deal with problems accordingly	1	2	3	4	5
Accept the situation and learn to live with it	1	2	3	4	5
Seek as much social support as possible e.g. from family, friends, Therapist, GP etc.	1	2	3	4	5
Unhelpful Behaviour					
'Staying busy'	5	4	3	2	1
'Bottling things up'	5	4	3	2	1
Using distractions (to take your mind off things)	5	4	3	2	1
Smoking more than usual	5	4	3	2	1
Delegate the problem	5	4	3	2	1
Drinking more alcohol than usual	5	4	3	2	1
Trying to hide away from the situation	5	4	3	2	1

Circle one number for each of the statements that apply to you. Then add up your scores and plot the total on the scale below. A score of 42 or higher is preferable. Examine your low-scoring items. Think about what you can do to improve these low scores.

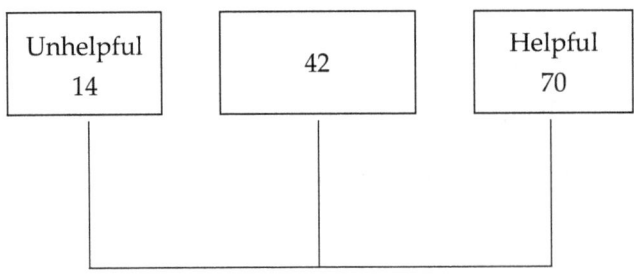

(Footnote: 3)

Relaxation Exercise

For a Quick Release of Tension

This is a breathing technique which can be beneficial in a difficult situation, as it helps your body to quickly feel relaxed. The emphasis is on controlled breathing.

1. Take several deep breaths in through your nose (deeper than usual) and push them out through your mouth quite forcefully.
   (This little phrase might be helpful – "smell the strawberries, blow out the candles".)

2. As you breathe in say to yourself "calm in".

3. As you breathe out say to yourself "tension out". At the same time, imagine the tension flowing out of your body.

4. Return to normal breathing for a few seconds

5. Repeat the exercise several times – until you feel calmer.

(Footnote: 4)

CHAPTER SIX

Homework from Session 1

1. Over the coming week, practise being aware of when your signs of stress are happening and note them down in your work diary. Put a star next to the stressful situation(s) in your diary, next to the appointment slot. You might be able to notice a pattern or highlight which specific situation(s) is/are causing you a lot of stress at work.

    It is also worth thinking about which symptoms occur first, as this could be used as an early warning sign. You can also note down how long the symptom or symptoms last; and exactly when, with whom and what is happening.

2. Think about which stressful situation, identified in your diary exercise, you would like to work on whilst going through this Programme.

3. Practise the relaxation exercise we've covered in this session.

Chapter Seven

Introduction to Session 2

In this session, you will be identifying your personal stress-inducing (i.e. stress creating) thinking errors and will use an effective technique to reduce and manage them. You will end this session by practising a stress reducing meditation exercise.

To begin, you will need to complete The 15 Thinking Errors – Self Audit and the Stress-Inducing Beliefs Indicator. This is so that you can identify your personal stress- inducing thinking errors and choose those you would like to work on. Once you have identified your personal thinking errors, you will need to decide on a stress provoking work issue you would like to address.

Some tables setting out the thought challenges or remedies to the 15 Thinking Errors will be provided together with some helpful challenging questions, also to help you change your negative thought processes to more positive enabling ones.

Instructions will be given on how to carry out a cognitive restructuring stress reducing technique (i.e. completion of the ABCDEF Challenging Stress-Inducing Thoughts Worksheet). Blank worksheets are provided for your use.

Go through the next few pages and complete the various worksheets.

CHAPTER SEVEN

SMART Programme – Session 2 – Overview

Name of Technique /Content/Activity	Purpose
The 15 Thinking Errors – Self Audit.	Cognitive: Tick those thinking errors which apply to you. These are areas which you will apply the techniques to, over the course of the SMART Programme and beyond.
Stress-Inducing Beliefs Indicator.	Cognitive: Identify those beliefs which apply to you. Again these are areas you will apply the techniques to.
Challenging Your Stress-Inducing Thoughts. The CBT, ABCDE Model of Stress.	Cognitive: See how the CBT Model of Stress can be used to manage and reduce stress. This is closely linked to the CBT theoretical basis of the SMART Programme.
Challenging the 15 Thinking Errors Exercise. The ABCDEF Challenging Stress-Inducing Thoughts Worksheet.	Cognitive: Information sheets listing 15 common thinking errors together with corresponding strategies to challenge or remedy each thinking error, are provided along with a list of helpful challenging questions. Instructions are given to enable you to carry out a cognitive restructuring activity – i.e. completion of the ABCDEF Challenging Stress-Inducing Thoughts Worksheet. You need to choose a stressful work situation or event to work on. This activity will enable you to produce a more helpful, stress-alleviating approach and thought pattern related to your stressful work situation.
Meditation Exercise.	Cognitive: Teaching you how to let go of your thoughts and relax.

(This is a long session and therefore does not have to be completed in one go).

The 15 Thinking Errors – Self Audit

Which stress-inducing and task–interfering beliefs do you have?
Think about previous or current stressful situations when completing this.

(Note down any of your own examples you can remember in the spaces provided)

Thinking Error	Have I ever experienced this before? ✓ or X	This happens in my stressful work situation(s). ✓
All or Nothing Thinking in absolutes or extremes. E.g. I <u>must</u> do all jobs well. That child is <u>always</u> bad. I <u>always</u> get things wrong.		
Labelling Globally rating ourselves and others instead of rating skills deficits or specific behaviours. E.g. I did a bad presentation. I'm totally useless. She's late again. She's so incompetent.		
Focusing on the negative Not keeping a balanced view on life or events. Only focusing on the negative things. E.g. Things are always going wrong in my lessons. That child is always causing problems.		
Discounting the positive Reframing anything positive as unimportant. E.g. When my manager praises my achievements she is only doing so to be nice.		
Mind reading Inferring from other people's behaviour that they are either thinking or responding negatively towards us. E.g. I'm sure my work colleagues think that I can't do this project successfully. The Head teacher has ignored me again. He must have seen me at the supermarket. What have I done to upset him?		

Chapter Seven

The 15 Thinking Errors – Self Audit		
Thinking Error	Have I ever experienced this before? ✓ or X	This happens in my stressful work situation(s). ✓
Fortune Telling Predicting the worst-case scenario, often without sufficient evidence. E.g. What's the point in trying? I'll never get promoted. It's always wet and muddy after I've washed the car.		
Magnification or 'Awfulising' Blowing events out of proportion. E.g. If I don't meet that deadline, the outcome will be terrible. If I have to move house, it will be the end of the world.		
Minimisation Condemning ourselves for our shortcomings and making excuses for our strengths or successes. E.g. The exams my students passed were the easy ones. I was lucky. Getting that job was nothing really.		
Emotional Reasoning Evaluating situations by how we feel. E.g. I feel so angry. This proves my boss treated me badly. I feel anxious, so this must be a nasty parent.		
Blame Blaming others for problems and not taking any personal responsibility. E.g. It's all the Head teacher's fault. She should see how busy I am. Where is my diary? Who has moved it?		
Over generalisation Predicting recurring outcomes on the basis of only one event. E.g. I've had a bad morning so the day is bound to get worse!		

The 15 Thinking Errors – Self Audit		
Thinking Error	Have I ever experienced this before? ✓ or X	This happens in my stressful work situation(s). ✓
Personalisation Blaming ourselves unfairly for things we are not totally responsible for. E.g. All my pupils did not achieve good grades. It's all my fault.		
Demanding-ness Holding unrealistic expectations or rigid and absolute beliefs. Usually expressed as 'oughts', 'have tos', 'got tos', 'shoulds' and 'musts'. E.g. I <u>must</u> perform well regardless of the lack of materials and required support. Children <u>should always</u> be perfectly behaved.		
Phoney-ism Fearing that others may find out that we are not the person we appear to be. E.g. Even though I have always been a good teacher, one day I'll make a mistake and they will discover how incompetent I really am.		
I-can't-stand-it-itis **(or I can't bear it)** Telling ourselves this, lowers our tolerance for dealing with setbacks or annoying situations. E.g. I can't bear taking assemblies. I can't stand noisy children.		

© Dr Paulette C. Ogun (2014) Adapted from Palmer & Cooper, 2007, pp. 49–50. (Published with permission)

Chapter Seven

As well as the 15 Thinking Errors, there are also stress-inducing beliefs which people can have. These beliefs are self-defeating, task-interfering and goal-blocking in nature.

Stress-Inducing Beliefs Indicator

Read the list of beliefs below and circle any which you hold strongly **(S)**, moderately strongly **(M)** or weakly **(W)**.

Researchers have found that if a person holds on strongly to one of the beliefs below, when an event occurs that does not live up to expectations, stress may result.

Note: 'shoulds', 'musts', 'have tos', 'got tos' and similar demanding ideas you may hold are interchangeable. So if instead of a 'should' you use a 'must', it still rates on this list.

1	S	M	W	Events should go smoothly.
2	S	M	W	Work must be exciting and stimulating.
3	S	M	W	If I lost my job, it would be awful.
4	S	M	W	If I lost my job, I could not bear it.
5	S	M	W	My job is one of the most important things to me.
6	S	M	W	I must perform well at all important tasks.
7	S	M	W	My work should be recognised by others.
8	S	M	W	I am indispensable at work.
9	S	M	W	I must enjoy myself whatever I am doing.
10	S	M	W	I must not get bored.
11	S	M	W	I should not encounter problems.
12	S	M	W	I should have the solitude I deserve.
13	S	M	W	I must escape from responsibilities and demands.
14	S	M	W	I should be treated fairly.
15	S	M	W	I should be treated as special.
16	S	M	W	I should be in control of all significant situations.
17	S	M	W	Others should respect me.
18	S	M	W	I should get on well with my friends and family.
19	S	M	W	My children should do well in life.
20	S	M	W	If things went badly, it would be awful.
21	S	M	W	If things went badly, I could not stand it.

22	S	M	W	Things never work out well for me.
23	S	M	W	If things go wrong, those responsible are stupid, useless, idiots or failures.
24	S	M	W	If I fail at a task, that proves I'm a failure or useless.
				Additional beliefs (write them in):
25	S	M	W	
26	S	M	W	

(Footnote: 5)

If you hold more than 10 strongly, it is very likely that you make many situations into potential stress scenarios! Even if you hold any of the above beliefs only moderately, under extremes of pressure you are likely to become quite stressed.

You might be able to think of some of your own. It's a good idea to note these down too as you might want to choose them to work on.

CHAPTER SEVEN

Challenging Your Stress-Inducing Thoughts

As noted in Chapter Four, Dr Albert Ellis, an internationally renowned Psychologist, worked out a sequence of events that lead to stress. They are similar to the first 3 stages of the CBT Model of Stress described in Session 1 (see Chapter 6). However he later added two more stages to it and called it the ABCDE Model of Stress. These extra stages (D and E) can be used to challenge and change our stress-inducing beliefs and thinking errors so that our stress levels are greatly reduced or completely gone. See his Model below:

The A B C D E Model of Stress

(By Dr Albert Ellis)

A. Activating event or situation

B. Beliefs about the event (it is perceived as stressful)

C. Consequences (stress response):
- Emotional e.g. anxiety, anger
- Behavioural e.g. aggression, avoidance
- Physiological e.g. palpitations, sweaty/clammy hands

D. Dispute the beliefs at 'B'

E. Effective new approach to deal with the activating event or problem at 'A'.

(Footnote: 6)

Thinking skills can be used to help you challenge inaccurate perceptions about events or the common 15 Thinking Errors.

We will now look at a chart of the 15 Thinking Errors with the corresponding challenges to remedy them. Read through them carefully.

There is also a list of helpful challenging questions which you can refer to. You can use them as a prompt sheet if needed. The main 3 things to remember about the helpful challenging questions are:

1. Is the belief logical? (Does it make logical sense?)

2. Is the belief realistic? (Is it happening in reality?)

3. Is the belief helpful in - reducing stress; accomplishing goals; and making the execution of tasks better?

(Footnote: 7)

Challenging the 15 Thinking Errors	
Thinking Error	**How to Challenge the Thinking Error**
All or Nothing Thinking in absolutes or extremes. E.g. I <u>must</u> do all jobs well. 　　That child is <u>always</u> bad. 　　I <u>always</u> get things wrong. 　　This <u>should</u> happen.	**Relative Thinking. Avoid thinking in absolute terms such as "must" and "should".** Be more realistic. Try to find a middle ground to help you keep the situation in perspective. **E.g.** I'll do a satisfactory job with the resources and time available to me. Although I've failed to reach 2 targets on time, I have successfully achieved 8 others (Instead of – I never reach my targets).
Labelling Globally rating ourselves and others instead of rating skills deficits or specific behaviours. E.g. I did a bad presentation. I'm totally useless. 　　She's late again. She's so incompetent.	**Befriend Yourself** Don't beat yourself/others up if you/they make a mistake. Treat yourself/them as you would a friend who had made a mistake. You would try to look for the positives. Describe the situation accurately. **E.g. Instead of** – That was a bad presentation. That proves I'm completely useless. **Be objective about the situation and describe it more accurately.** Although some aspects of my presentation were not very good, <u>this does not mean</u> that I'm completely useless. In fact I know what areas to improve on next time.
	De-labelling Avoid globally rating yourself or others **e.g.** As "useless", "stupid" or a "total failure". <u>Instead focus on the behavioural or skill deficit being displayed</u>. **E.g.** OK some things have gone wrong in my job. I can survive this hassle. This does not mean things are always going wrong. This, that and the other went quite well. **When another person makes you angry** – again <u>rate the behaviour not the person</u>. **E.g.** Although Tom has concentration difficulties, that does not make him a totally awful child. He has X & Y good points. Although my manager has interpersonal skills deficits, it does not make him a total idiot. (You might then do something behaviourally about this, such as use assertiveness skills.)

Chapter Seven

Challenging the 15 Thinking Errors	
Thinking Error	**How to Challenge the Thinking Error**
Focusing on the negative Not keeping a balanced view of life or events. Only focusing on the negative things. E.g. Things are always going wrong in my lessons. That child is always causing problems.	**Broaden the picture** Instead of focusing on the negative and discounting the positive, start concentrating on more realistic and positive aspects of a situation. Don't blame yourself (personalisation) or innocent bystanders. **If blame arises** (i.e. if you blame yourself or others): 1. Write down all the different people or factors involved. 2. Draw a circle on a large sheet of paper. 3. Create a **pie diagram** from the circle, with each section being roughly equal to the amount of fault or responsibility of the different people or factors involved. 4. Lastly, whatever is left of the pie diagram is likely to be your responsibility. This is a good technique to use to analyse why something went wrong – such as with a work project. **E.g.** You were told about it half way to the deadline; you didn't have enough resources to complete certain sections; you had another more important deadline to meet just before this new project which went wrong; you didn't tell your line manager about the first deadline, so became overloaded; you were not allocated admin support etc.
Discounting the positive Reframing anything positive as unimportant. E.g. When my manager praises my achievements she is only doing so to be nice.	**Broaden the picture.** Concentrate on the real and positive aspects of a situation. **E.g.** I really did do a good piece of work which was helpful for the school or child in this way etc. **Befriend yourself.** Talk to yourself as if you were a friend. **E.g.** Reassure yourself that you have performed well and do deserve success, praise etc.

Challenging the 15 Thinking Errors	
Thinking Error	**How to Challenge the Thinking Error**

Mind reading
 	
Inferring from other people's behaviour that they are either thinking or responding negatively towards us.
 	
E.g.:
 	
    I'm sure my work colleagues think that I can't do this project successfully.
 	
    The Head teacher has ignored me again. He must have seen me at the supermarket. What have I done to upset him?
	Seek Evidence. Avoid mind reading or making assumptions
	
	E.g. You can ask family, friends or colleagues for feedback about the work you have done. You can also ask your manager, partner, neighbour etc. - directly, if you think they are not happy about something you have done.

Fortune Telling Predicting the worst-case scenario, often without sufficient evidence. E.g. What's the point in trying? I'll never get promoted. It's always wet and muddy after I've washed the car.	**Seek Evidence** Rather than predict the worst and cause yourself unnecessary stress, wait and see what actually happens. You can also prepare for any eventualities –noting the phrase "Expect the best, prepare for the worst" (but not over-preparing). Also, look back in the past to similar events. Did the worst happen? If it did, are you still alive to tell the tale? **Think Flexibly** Dogmatic, inflexible, absolutist and demanding beliefs trigger high levels of stress. **E.g.** I <u>must</u> do well during this OFSTED inspection. **Instead introduce flexible beliefs** such as preferences, desires and wants. **E.g.** It's strongly preferable to perform well, but realistically I can only do my best. If I perform well and show I can move up to the next level, it is possible that I can get promoted, although nothing is guaranteed. If I don't get promoted on this occasion, I can always try again another time – after working on the points of weakness highlighted.

Chapter Seven

Challenging the 15 Thinking Errors	
Thinking Error	**How to Challenge the Thinking Error**
Magnification or 'Awfulising' Blowing events out of proportion. E.g. If I don't meet that deadline, the outcome will be terrible. If I have to move house, it will be the end of the world.	**Demagnify or 'Deawfulise'** Step back from stressful situations and look at them dispassionately, as if they are happening to somebody else. This will allow you to distance yourself from your immediate stress-inducing thinking so you can think more clearly. Seldom are things "the end of the world". They might be a hassle or inconvenience. No more, no less. Be realistic about exactly what has happened. **E.g.** I didn't get the job. It's a hassle. Too bad. (No one has died – to put it into perspective).
Minimisation Condemning ourselves for our shortcomings and making excuses for our strengths or successes. E.g. The exams my students passed were the easy ones. I was lucky. Getting that job was nothing really.	**Broaden the picture**. Be realistic, noting things in real and positive terms. E.g. So I did badly on X and Y but I did really well on A, B and C. **Or** – I prepared my students thoroughly for those exams, so I helped them pass. I should be pleased with myself. **Befriend yourself.** Talk to yourself as if you were a friend. **E.g.** Reassure yourself that you have performed well and do deserve success, praise etc.
Emotional Reasoning Evaluating situations by how we feel. E.g. I feel so angry. This proves my boss treated me badly. I feel anxious, so this must be a nasty parent.	**Keep Emotions in their place** Tell yourself that just because you feel a certain way, it does not mean this matches the situation.
Blame Blaming others for problems and not taking any personal responsibility. E.g. It's all the Head Teacher's fault. She should see how busy I am. Where is my diary? Who has moved it?	**Broaden the picture** (See the section about the pie diagram above.)

Challenging the 15 Thinking Errors	
Thinking Error	**How to Challenge the Thinking Error**
Over generalisation Predicting recurring outcomes on the basis of only one event. E.g. I've had a bad morning so the day is bound to get worse!	**Challenge this realistically** **Look for evidence in real life.** Rather than stressing out, wait and see if this really happens as you have predicted. **Also look for evidence in the past.** Has this or something similar happened in the past on a repeated basis? If not, it is highly unlikely to be the case in the future.
Personalisation Blaming ourselves unfairly for things we are not totally responsible for. E.g. All my pupils did not achieve good grades. It's all my fault.	**Broaden the picture** (See the section about the pie diagram above.)
Demanding-ness Holding unrealistic expectations or rigid and absolute beliefs. Usually expressed as 'oughts', 'have tos', 'got tos', 'shoulds' and 'musts'. E.g. I <u>must</u> perform well regardless of the lack of materials and required support. Children <u>should always</u> be perfectly behaved.	**Think more Flexibly** Dogmatic, inflexible, absolutist and demanding beliefs trigger high levels of stress. Think in terms of preferences, desires and wants. **E.g.** Although it's highly preferable to achieve my deadlines, I can only do my best, given the lack of materials and required support. I would prefer children to behave well all of the time but recognise that they may misbehave now and again as nobody is perfect.

Chapter Seven

Challenging the 15 Thinking Errors	
Thinking Error	**How to Challenge the Thinking Error**
Phoney-ism Fearing that others may find out that we are not the person we appear to be. E.g. Even though I have always been a good teacher, one day I'll make a mistake and they will discover how incompetent I really am.	**Befriend yourself.** Reassure yourself as you would a friend. E.g. One or two mistakes are not going to change the competent picture you have built up for yourself over the years. **Seek evidence.** Ask trusted friends, colleagues and family about their perceptions of you. **Broaden the picture.** Be realistic about your skills and the positive aspects of yourself. **Deawfulise.** Step back and look at things dispassionately. E.g. Even if I did make a mistake, that's all it would be, no more no less. The fact that I've taught well for so many years shows that I'm clearly competent. Anyone can make a mistake.
I-can't-stand-it-itis (or I can't bear it) Telling ourselves this, lowers our tolerance for dealing with setbacks or annoying situations. E.g. I can't bear taking assemblies. I can't stand noisy children.	**Think more Flexibly and Realistically.** E.g. Some times will be better than others. **Seek evidence.** Ask friends, family and colleagues about what they perceive of you in the given scenario. **Challenge behaviourally.** Put yourself in the situation. E.g. For – I can't bear doing assemblies – take an assembly as living proof that you can "bear" it.

© Dr Paulette C. Ogun (2014) Adapted from Palmer & Cooper, 2007 (Published with permission)

The stress reducing activity which we will go through next, follows Dr Ellis's ABCDE Model of Stress, with an <u>additional level F</u>. Palmer and Cooper (2007) have added the level F. The level F means to remain <u>focused on the existing task or problem</u> and to also think about the <u>future focus.</u> In other words, at level F you are also thinking about what you have learnt from the ABCDE process, which can be remembered and used in the future, the next time a similar problem occurs.

Before starting the activity (of completing the ABCDEF Challenging Stress-Inducing Thoughts Worksheet), I will set out a list of helpful challenging questions (Palmer & Cooper, 2007, pp. 60-61 – published with permission) which you can use alongside the remedial thought challenges to the 15 Thinking Errors.

Helpful Challenging Questions
1. Is it logical?
2. Would a scientist agree with my logic?
3. Where is the evidence for my belief?
4. Where is the belief written (apart from inside my own head)?
5. Is my belief realistic?
6. Would my friends and colleagues agree with my idea?
7. Does everybody share my attitude? If not, why not?
8. Am I expecting myself or others to be perfect, as opposed to fallible, human beings?
9. What makes the situation so awful, terrible or horrible?
10. Am I making a mountain out of a molehill?
11. Will it seem this bad in 1, 3, 6, or 12 months' time?
12. Will it be important in 2 years' time?
13. Is it really as bad a problem as a serious accident or a close bereavement?
14. Am I exaggerating the importance of this problem?
15. Am I fortune-telling again, with little evidence that the worst-case scenario will actually happen?
16. If I 'can't stand it' or 'can't bear it', what will really happen?
17. If I can't stand it, will I really fall apart?
18. Am I concentrating on my (or others') weaknesses and neglecting my (or others') strengths?
19. Am I agonising about how things should be instead of dealing with them as they are?
20. Where is this thought or attitude getting me?
21. Is my belief helping me to attain my goal(s)?
22. Is my belief goal-focused and problem-solving?
23. If a friend made a similar mistake, would I be so critical?
24. Am I thinking in all-or-nothing terms? Is there any middle ground?
25. Am I labelling myself, somebody or something else? Is this logical and a fair thing to do?
26. Just because a problem has occurred, does it mean that I am/it is/ they are stupid, a failure, useless or hopeless?
27. Am I placing demands (such as 'should' or 'musts') on myself or others? If I am, is this proving helpful and constructive?
28. Am I taking things too personally?
29. Am I blaming others unfairly just to make myself (temporarily) feel better?"

CHAPTER SEVEN

How to Use the Helpful Challenging Questions to Complete the ABCDEF Challenging Stress-Inducing Thoughts Worksheet

Choose the questions that may help you to challenge your **B**eliefs at **B** on the ABCDEF Challenging Stress-Inducing Thoughts Worksheet, overleaf. It is important to ask yourself the questions and then think through the potential answers for a while.

Once you have asked yourself the relevant questions, change the belief you held at **B** to one that is more reasonable, realistic and beneficial. E.g. Try to move your attitude from "Missing the deadline is a catastrophe" to "Missing the deadline is a nuisance, but hardly a catastrophe. I'm blowing this way out of proportion!" (This is a realistic and beneficial stress-reducing belief). Note down this new belief in column **D**.

Now note down your Effective new approach to dealing with the situation, at **E**.

E.g. "Stop procrastinating and wasting time. Create a Gantt chart and 'To Do' list for completing the task and start work immediately."

At **F**, which is for Focus – i.e. staying focused on the current problem and also for the future focus - note down what you will remember the next time a similar problem occurs.

Instructions for Completion of the ABCDEF Challenging Stress-Inducing Thoughts Worksheet.

Complete the worksheet in the following order:

A. Think of the stressful situation (i.e. the **A**ctivating event or situation) – note it at A. Your goal is what you would like to achieve.

C. Note down your **C**onsequential behaviour and emotions as a result of feeling stressed, at C. E.g. procrastinating, anxious.

B. Imagine the situation and get into the feeling. Write down all your stress-inducing thoughts (SITs) or **B**eliefs at B. (These are the stress-producing thoughts.)

D. Dispute or challenge your stress-inducing thoughts – using the remedial thoughts information supplied above (i.e. "Challenging the 15 Thinking Errors" and the list of "Helpful Challenging Questions"). You are now creating some stress-alleviating thoughts (SATs) which are stress-reducing thoughts. Write these down at D.

E. Think of a practical **E**ffective thing you can do to deal with the activating stressful event/ situation. Write this down at E.

F. Stay **F**ocussed on the existing problem AND in particular, write down at F what you have learned from this situation that can be remembered for a similar problem in the Future.

An example of a completed worksheet is provided below.

A Completed Example of the ABCDEF Challenging Stress-Inducing Thoughts Worksheet.

Case Study – John the Procrastinating Perfectionist. (His completed worksheet.)

(Order in which sheet was completed = A, C, B, D, E, F)

Activating event or situation A	Beliefs Stress-inducing thoughts (SITs) or beliefs B	Consequences C	Disputing the beliefs at B Stress-alleviating thoughts (SATs) D	Effective new approach to deal with the activating event E	Focus and Future Lessons F
Giving a presentation at work. **Goal**: To do a good presentation.	I'm going to screw up (fortune telling).	Anxious and stressed.	How do I know if I'm going to screw up? I'm not clairvoyant!	I need to focus now on preparation of the presentation. This will give me a better chance of success.	The lesson for the future is to realise that I could become a lot better at presentations if I stop avoiding them. In future start to use Coping Imagery to help me deal with potential problems.
	I must give a good presentation (demands upon self).	Anxious and worried; pro-crastinates.	It's strongly preferable to give a good presentation but I don't have to.	Stop pro-crastinating. Make a priority list of what I need to do. Do, don't stew!	
	It will be terrible if I screw up (awfulising).	Anxious and stressed.	In reality, I doubt that the world will stop. I'm unlikely to lose my job.	Stay focused on the task.	
	They will think I'm totally useless (labelling and mind reading).	A bit low.	I've spent years avoiding giving presentations, so I need more practice. However, if I do screw up it doesn't mean I'm totally useless. It just means that I lack presentation skills – not a big deal.	I'll use evaluation forms so I can really find out what they think.	

(Footnote: 8)

CHAPTER SEVEN

See two blank ABCDEF Challenging Stress-Inducing Thoughts Worksheets below for you to complete. This is a cognitive restructuring method of stress reduction. Remember that you will be working on your chosen stressful work scenario using the "Challenging the 15 Thinking Errors" tables and the list of "Helpful Challenging Questions", provided above.

The ABCDEF Challenging Stress-Inducing Thoughts Worksheet

(Order in which sheet is to be completed = A, C, B, D, E, F)

Activating event or situation A	Beliefs Stress-inducing thoughts (SITs) or beliefs B	Consequences C	Disputing the beliefs at B Stress-alleviating thoughts (SATs) D	Effective new approach to deal with the activating event E	Focus and Future lessons F
Event: Your Goal:					

(Footnote: 8)

The ABCDEF Challenging Stress-Inducing Thoughts Worksheet

(Order in which sheet is to be completed = A, C, B, D, E, F)

Activating event or situation A	Beliefs Stress-inducing thoughts (SITs) or beliefs B	Consequences C	Disputing the beliefs at B Stress-alleviating thoughts (SATs) D	Effective new approach to deal with the activating event E	Focus and Future lessons F
Event: Your Goal:					

(Footnote: 8)

CHAPTER SEVEN

Meditation Exercise – Letting Go of Thoughts

This exercise is highly structured and is found in many cultures in one form or another. During this exercise you passively watch the flow of your feelings, perceptions and thoughts, one after another, without being concerned about how they are connected to one another or their meaning. This will allow you to view what's on your mind and then let it go away.

1. Find your posture and centre yourself. Take several deep breaths.

Finding Your Posture

Carry out points A to D below.

A. Select <u>one</u> of the following positions which is most comfortable for you:

- In a chair with your knees comfortably apart, your legs uncrossed, and your hands resting in your lap.

- Cross-legged on the floor. This position is most comfortable and stable when a cushion is placed under your bottom so that both knees touch the floor.

B. Sit with your back straight (but not ramrod rigid) and let the weight of your head rest directly on your spinal column. This can be achieved by pulling in your chin slightly. Allow the small of your back to arch.

C. Rock briefly from side to side, then from front to back, and establish the point at which your upper torso feels balanced on your hips.

D. Close your mouth and breathe through your nose. Place your tongue on the roof of your mouth.

How to Centre Yourself

Being centred means intentionally keeping an area of calmness within yourself by conscious thought, no matter how fiercely your emotions might be swirling. For that reason, being centred is sometimes compared to being the eye in the centre of a tornado.

A helpful way to centre yourself is to close your eyes and take several deep breaths. Notice the quality of your breathing. Is it fast or slow? Deep or shallow? Notice where your breath rests in your body. Is it up high in your chest or down low in your belly? Try moving it around from one area of your body to another. Breathe into your upper chest, then into your stomach and then drop your breath into your lower belly. Feel your abdomen expand and contract as the air goes in and out. Notice how the upper chest and stomach areas seem almost still. This "dropped breath" is the most relaxing stance to meditate from. However, if you find it difficult to take deep belly breaths, don't worry. Your breath will drop by itself as you become more practiced in meditation.

2. Once you have found your posture and centred yourself as above, close your eyes and visualize yourself sitting at the bottom of a deep pool of water. When you have a perception, thought or feeling, see it as a bubble and let it ascend away from you and vanish. When it is gone, wait for the next one to emerge and repeat the process. Don't think about what is in the bubble. Just look at it. Sometimes the same bubble may come up lots of times, or several bubbles will seem related to each other, or the bubbles may contain nothing. That's fine. Don't allow yourself to be bothered by these thoughts. Just observe them pass in front of your mind's eye.

3. If you feel uncomfortable imagining being under water, imagine that you are sitting by the side of a river, observing a leaf drift slowly downstream. Imagine the leaf being one perception, thought or feeling and then let it drift out of sight. Return to looking at the river, waiting for the next leaf to float by with a new thought. Or, if you wish, you can imagine your thoughts ascending in puffs of smoke from a campfire.

The practise of meditation can bring discernment, focus and a sense of rejuvenation to your life.

As you develop in your practise of meditation and it becomes easier, you will find yourself wanting to lengthen your time doing it. However, in terms of relaxation, 20 to 30 minutes once or twice a day is enough to achieve this.

(Footnote: 9)

CHAPTER SEVEN

Homework from Session 2

1. Read through what has been covered in this session, to cement it in your minds.

2. Practise the remedial stress-alleviating thoughts and/or actions you have worked out using the ABCDEF Challenging Stress-Inducing Thoughts Worksheet.

3. Practise the meditation exercise.

Chapter Eight

Introduction to Session 3

In this session, we are going to look at a shortened quicker cognitive method of reducing stressful thoughts – The Stress Thought Record. We will also look at managing and reducing anger which is the 'fight' response to a stressful situation (referring to the 'fight-flight' reaction which is activated by dangerous or stressful situations). Then the use of imagery as a stress reducing tool will be introduced. The issue of self-esteem will also be examined, as one's concept of self-esteem can lead to a vulnerability to stress.

CHAPTER EIGHT

SMART Programme – Session 3 - Overview

Name of Technique/ Content/Activity	Purpose
Stress Thought Record	Cognitive: Using the strategies already provided in Session 2 (e.g. Challenging the 15 Thinking Errors), you are taught this new cognitive restructuring technique. A worked example is provided with instructions. You then carry out an activity using the strategy – looking at a personal work-based stressor.
Managing Anger	Cognitive: Using the strategies already provided in Session 2 (e.g. Helpful Challenging Questions), you are taught a format, like the Stress Thought Record above, which can be used to identify anger-activating thoughts for specific situations. These can then be challenged and replaced with more helpful/enabling thoughts. You can also think of other constructive actions that you can take.
Coping Imagery	Cognitive: You are taught a new cognitive strategy for identifying and changing stressful thoughts around an upcoming stressful event and a method of mentally rehearsing for the event – practising overcoming your fears.
Self-Motivation Imagery	Cognitive: You are taught how to use imagery to get yourself out of a procrastination rut.
Time Projection Imagery	Cognitive: You are taught how to use imagery to help put a current stressful work situation into perspective. The aim is to help you to reduce your stress levels regarding that situation.
Self-esteem	Cognitive: You will be able to consider what is important to you in your life (e.g. being a successful career person; having a nice house; always getting the promotion you go for etc.) and how this may impact on your self-esteem. You will be able to identify negative/unhelpful beliefs or thoughts and challenge these. Self-acceptance, faults and all, is an important stress reducing mentality.
Relaxation Imagery	Cognitive and Behavioural: You will learn a relaxation exercise using imagery. The aim is to produce physiological relaxation as well as to reduce stressful thoughts.

Stress Thought Record

For some stress-triggering situations there is no need to use the 6-column ABCDEF Challenging Stress-Inducing Thoughts Worksheet, used in Session 2. With practise, you can 'cut to the chase' by using a 2-column Stress Thought Record instead.

To use the Stress Thought Record you need to make a note of the stress-inducing thoughts (SITs) or thinking errors you are having for a particular problem or issue. Once you have identified which SITs are creating your stress or making it worse, you can apply the relevant remedial ways of thinking and challenging questions provided in Session 2 to create stress-alleviating thoughts (SATs).

(The SITs and SATs method was developed by Neenan and Palmer, at the Centre for Stress Management – see Palmer and Cooper, 2007, pp. 68-70).

A completed example of how this works is provided below.

Stress Thought Record

Example:

Problem: Possible redundancy	**Goal:** To reduce my stress levels and deal with financial concerns
Stress-Inducing Thoughts (SITs)	**Stress-Alleviating Thoughts (SATs)**
Redundancy could impact upon my family finances	Worrying won't decrease the likelihood of redundancy - it will probably make it worse if anything. I have lots of skills – if I was made redundant I shouldn't have too much of a problem finding other employment.
This shouldn't happen to me.	Why shouldn't it? The reality is that cutbacks may have to be made.
The company should look after its staff.	The company has everyone to consider – it's not personal to me.
They are treating me so badly after all the years I've worked for them.	Are they? I'm taking this rather personally. It won't help me!
	Other ideas: When worry occurs at work, tell myself that, "there's nothing I can do about it right now." Perhaps use 10 minutes worry time in the evening before dinner. Use problem-solving skills to work on my employment situation and revise my financial situation. Ask for a break in mortgage payments. Update my CV and scan the papers for jobs.

(Footnote: 10)

Chapter Eight

Now complete the blank Stress Thought Record below, working on the stressful situation or issue you have chosen to focus on. Remember to use the helpful thinking skills provided in Session 2 to create your stress-alleviating thoughts. An extra blank Record is provided for your use.

Here are the instructions for completing the Stress Thought Record.

Completing a Stress Thought Record to Combat Stress

Instructions

1. Think of the situation or event you are stressed about. Note down the problem on the blank Stress Thought Record provided.

2. Note down on the Stress Thought Record your goal or goals which relate to this problem.

3. Now think about the problem. When you are becoming stressed about it what are you telling yourself? Note down these stress-inducing thoughts in the first column.

4. Now think of the more helpful alternatives (i.e. stress-alleviating thoughts (SATs)) to the stress-inducing thoughts (SITs). Note the SATs down opposite to the corresponding SITs in the second column.

5. Once you have finished developing the SATs, note down any additional ideas or specific tasks or strategies to help you to achieve your desired goals.

Stress Thought Record

Problem:	Goal:
Stress-Inducing Thoughts (SITs)	**Stress-Alleviating Thoughts (SATs)**
	Other ideas/goal achieving actions:

(Footnote: 11)

Chapter Eight

Stress Thought Record

Problem:	Goal:
Stress-Inducing Thoughts (SITs)	**Stress-Alleviating Thoughts (SATs)**
	Other ideas/goal achieving actions:

(Footnote: 11)

Managing Anger

Being overly angry can be another symptom of stress. This is because it is the stress "fight" emotional response in contrast to anxiety, which is the stress "flight" emotional response.

Being overly angry can cause problems as it may cause you to respond inappropriately, which can lead to other difficulties. For example, an angry outburst at work could lead to disciplinary difficulties or parental complaints about how their child was handled by you, their teacher. Angry outbursts could also lead to a relationship breakdown between you and your spouse/partner or you and your children. In addition, being overly angry can be detrimental to your health and can lead to health problems like high blood pressure, which has the potential to put you at risk of having a stroke.

Hence, it is important to have techniques which can help you to manage and reduce your anger, especially if you feel it is beginning to have a detrimental effect on your relationships and your ability to focus on projects or tasks.

In managing your anger, it is important to accept the fallibility of others although you don't accept or excuse their behaviour. Instead of globally rating them as:

- "Totally useless."
- "The lazy so and so."
- "A complete waste of space."
- "Stupid."
- "Complete idiot."
- "xxxxxx!"

Rate <u>aspects</u> as follows:

- On this occasion this pupil acted stupidly but this does not mean he is stupid.
- This is more evidence that he is fallible.
- That parent has interpersonal skills deficits.
- My manager is exhibiting many management skills deficits.

The next technique uses a similar format to the Stress Thought Record in that it involves you identifying your anger-activating thoughts and replacing or countering them with anger-deactivating thoughts.

If you can identify anger as a stress symptom you need to address, try doing the following activity. A completed example/case study is given first, followed by a blank sheet for you to use.

Chapter Eight

Case Study: Angry Peter

Peter was becoming very angry with his colleagues, who he believed were not 'pulling their weight' on a particular project. With his coach, Simon, he noted down his anger-activating thoughts on a worksheet (see below) and then with the help of his coach he developed alternative anger-deactivating thoughts. Once they had finished this, they then developed constructive ideas and included them in the worksheet.

Anger-Activating Thoughts	Anger-Deactivating Thoughts
Why don't they pull their weight?	Perhaps I'm over-generalising
They don't care about the project.	Just because they are not always talking about the project, it does not mean that they don't care.
We will get the project in late.	I'll go over the schedule again and check whether we are all keeping to our agreed deadlines.
I can't stand their inefficiency.	If they have been inefficient, I've stood it for the past two years!
They really should focus on this project.	At the meetings they seem focused.
They are complete idiots.	It's not true. They wouldn't have their qualifications and their jobs if they were complete idiots.
	Other constructive ideas: Perhaps I'm over-reacting.
	Am I taking this project too seriously?
	I'll discuss my concerns in a calm manner at the next team meeting and get people's feedback.

(Footnote: 12)

Deactivating Your Anger – Exercise

Instructions: Think of a situation or person (or both!) that you feel angry about. Note down on the worksheet the anger-activating thoughts and/or images that you have, and then develop alternative anger-deactivating thoughts so you feel less angry and stressed and more task-focused instead. Include additional constructive ideas too, that may help you to deal with the problem.

Useful tip: It may be helpful to ask a colleague or friend you trust (and who does not seem to get wound up about issues) to help you work out the anger-deactivating thoughts.

Anger-Activating Thoughts	Anger-Deactivating Thoughts
	Other constructive ideas:

(Footnote: 13)

The above activity for managing your anger is mostly a cognitive one. There are other behavioural methods which can also be used. For example, you could use a physical relaxation exercise, such as the Quick Release of Tension breathing technique which we practised in the first session, or you could become more assertive.

Use of Imagery to Reduce Stress Levels

There are a variety of imagery techniques you can use to reduce and manage your stress levels. I will share some of the most effective ones with you here.

Before explaining how they work I will outline their benefits:

- Coping Imagery – very effective in reducing stress by helping you deal with potentially stressful upcoming events. It can even help with extreme issues such as phobias.

- Self-Motivation Imagery – helps you motivate yourself to achieve your goals.

- Time Projection Imagery – helps you de-awfulise situations.

- Relaxation Imagery – very effective in helping you achieve a relaxed state of mind and body.

Coping Imagery

This involves you identifying your worst fears about a situation and thinking of practical ways to deal with them. You can elicit the help of friends, colleagues or family members for coping ideas.

Once you have thought of practical coping ideas, you then find a quiet place, close your eyes and imagine your worst fears occurring and you dealing with them successfully. By doing this you are directly challenging the negative imagery that is causing you to worry and stress about a situation or event. Coping is the important word, as nothing is perfect. It allows you to be realistic in accepting that you may not give the perfect presentation or answers at an interview. However, now you have a way to effectively deal with any mistakes that may occur.

Coping Imagery helps you to face your worst fears and rehearse overcoming them, should they arise – thus significantly reducing your stress levels.

Examples of when Coping Imagery can be used are – before presentations at work, before job interviews and before teaching a difficult class. Teachers can help students to use this technique where they are particularly stressed about an upcoming exam.

Here are the instructions for using Coping Imagery:

Coping Imagery

Instructions

Step 1. Think of a future situation that you are stressed about.

Step 2. Note down the aspects of the situation that you are most stressed about.

Step 3. Develop ways to deal with these difficulties.

Step 4. Now carefully visualise yourself in the feared situation. Slowly picture yourself coping with each anticipated difficulty as it arises.

   Repeat this procedure 3 or 4 times.

Step 5. Practice Step 4 daily, especially when you become stressed about the forthcoming event.

(Footnote: 14)

Using the instructions above, carry out the following activity:

Activity: Think of something stressful happening in your teaching week. E.g. You are a form tutor and you are running late for morning registration. What could you do? (Using your own issue is better.) Close your eyes and spend around 5 minutes going through your solution.

Self-Motivation Imagery

This is useful when a person wants to kick themselves into action. This technique was developed by Palmer and Neenan at the Centre for Coaching in London, who found that many of their clients avoided life changes because they feared that they would not be able to cope with the stress created.

It is provided here for you to use as required, now or in the future.

Chapter Eight

The instructions for using Self-Motivation Imagery are set out below:

Self-Motivation Imagery

Instructions

Spend a few minutes thinking about possible areas of your life that you could improve by taking actions that you have avoided. Examples may include: changing your job or going for promotion; returning to study; ending a significant relationship; writing a book; or challenging your manager, partner, parents or in-laws about some important issue. If you are unemployed, have you become disillusioned after receiving many 'rejections'?

Assuming you are not too depressed about the areas of life you would like to change, carry out the exercise below. Once you start, it is important to work through all three steps.

Step 1. Visualise the rest of your life not having undertaken the change that you would like to make. To assist in this exercise, imagine the effect upon yourself, and perhaps on significant others too, for the rest of your life until the day you die, if you do absolutely nothing. Think of your regrets, too. Imagine the effect year by year.

Step 2. Now visualise yourself undertaking what you want to do, and then see the short and long-term positive benefits of the change to you, and possibly others.

Step 3. Now consider how you are going to put Step 2 into action.

It is important that Step 1 (known as 'Inaction Imagery') is visualised before Step 2 (known as 'Action Imagery'), otherwise it is possible you may demotivate yourself, which is not the intention of the exercise!

Motivation Imagery has helped to change people's lives and pull them out of a boring, stressful rut into a new and exciting domain.

(Footnote: 15)

Time Projection Imagery

Time Projection Imagery is very useful to use when a person is going through a particularly stressful time, such as during a divorce, or if they have lost their job or when they have failed an exam. At these times it can be difficult to deal with things in a constructive manner and it is easy to lose sight of one's goals. Time Projection Imagery helps to put things into perspective and is therefore an effective deawfulising tool. It involves picturing yourself at various points in the future and thinking about whether the issue will be just as important or stressful then, as it is now.

It is provided here for you to use as required, now or in the future.

The instructions are below:

Time Projection Imagery

Instructions

Step 1. Think of a current problem or situation that you are stressed about.

Step 2. Picture yourself 3 months in the future.
Will the current problem be as stressful as it is now?

Step 3. Picture yourself 6 months in the future.
Will the current problem be as stressful or as important as it is now? Can you see yourself getting on with your life?

Step 4. Picture yourself 12 months in the future.
Will the current problem be as stressful or as important as it is now? Can you see yourself getting on with your life?

Step 5. Picture yourself 2 years in the future.
Will the current problem be as stressful or as important as it is now?
Will you laugh at your problem when you look back at it? Can you see yourself having fun again?

Step 6. Picture yourself 5 years in the future.
Will the memory and significance of the problem fade into the past?
If you still find it difficult to imagine a positive future, picture having a new job or career, different friends, or whatever is appropriate.

(Footnote: 16)

Self-Esteem vs. Self-Acceptance

Your self esteem belief system can be another source of stress.

Activity: Take a few minutes to note down on a sheet of paper how you build up your self-esteem, starting with "I'm OK because…" Then continue reading.

Did you say the following phrases to yourself – "I'm OK because…I have a successful career…I live in a lovely house…I have a happy marriage…I have high achieving children…I am a good parent…I am attractive."

If you did, you may be in the self-esteem trap. Here's why -

Research has found that one of the main causes of stress for people of all ages, especially in Western society, is having a strong belief in the traditional concept of self-esteem, which is based on external factors and concrete terms, such as achievements or ownership. This means that if these factors are lost or if things go wrong in those areas, the person's sense of self-worth and their self-esteem goes down.

You can change the way you develop your self-esteem by exchanging the traditional basis of self-esteem for self-acceptance!

IT IS MUCH BETTER TO ACCEPT YOURSELF AS YOU ARE.

Useful self-acceptance phrases are:

- "I'm OK simply because I exist."

- "I can accept myself, faults and all."

- "I would prefer to be better at or improve my skills in X and Y areas but realistically I don't have to."

- "I've failed at X. This does not mean that I'm a total failure (an unhelpful global self-rating) but that I lack skills in X and Y which I might be able to improve with more practice."

In this way, it is better to rate your skills or certain aspects of yourself in realistic terms than to do a global unrealistic rating. Also avoid "I should, must, ought to" etc. Instead talk of preferences, wants, like tos and even strong desires. This helps the concept of self-acceptance to remain realistic unlike the traditional approach to self-esteem. Avoid rigid perfectionism – which leads to dissatisfaction with yourself and others' performance.

Note: The rating of skills leads to healthy and realistic disappointment if you fail or perform badly but still retains motivation. For example, "I didn't get promoted this time because I am absolutely useless" can result from a self-esteem global rating based on being a high achiever, if you fail to achieve on a given occasion. Instead, it is much more helpful and realistic to say, "I am a pretty skilful person but I'm not perfect and I accept myself the way I am. On this occasion I lacked some of the skills required for the post. I can get some additional training for the next opportunity which comes along."

The concept of self-acceptance as a basis for self-esteem and self-worth is more robust than the traditional basis for self-esteem. Self-acceptance is realistic, logical and pragmatic. It helps people to have a sense of personal freedom and can reduce stress.

Relaxation Imagery

As noted above, the Relaxation Imagery technique is excellent for achieving a relaxed state of mind and body. It involves picturing in your mind, one of your favourite relaxing places (real or imaginary) and imagining being there in detail. Examples of some favourite relaxing places are, by the sea, taking a relaxing bath and walking in the countryside.

The instructions are below. Read them through and try it out:

Relaxation Imagery

Instructions

Step 1. Find a quiet place where you are unlikely to be disturbed. If possible, reduce the level of lighting.

Step 2. Find a comfortable position and lie down or sit quietly.

Step 3. Close your eyes and picture one of your favourite relaxing places.

Step 4. Focus on the colours in your relaxing place.

Step 5. Focus on one colour in particular.

Step 6. Focus on the sounds or silence in your relaxing place.

Step 7. Imagine touching something in your relaxing place.

Step 8. Focus on any aromas or smells in your relaxing place.

Step 9. In your own time, open your eyes.

Anyone who regularly practises this method will be able to achieve a relaxed state relatively quickly and with little effort. If you are really keen to master this Relaxation Imagery technique, it is recommended that you practise it twice a day for 14 days. After this amount of practice you will discover that you will be able to switch into it with ease. Many people have learnt to use this method with their eyes open while standing on crowded city trains, but this does take practice!

(Footnote: 17)

Note: The instructions for all the imagery techniques given above can be recorded, if this helps you remember what to do whilst carrying out the activity. For example, you could record them on your mobile phone or tablet and then play them back to yourself or you could ask a friend or family member to read the instructions out for you.

Chapter Eight

Homework from Session 3

1. Practise the stress-alleviating thoughts which you worked out using the Stress Thought Record.

2. If relevant, practise the anger-deactivating thoughts which you worked out during the Anger Management exercise.

3. Practise one of the imagery techniques, whichever is most relevant to you at the present time.

4. Practise the Relaxation Imagery exercise.

Chapter Nine

Introduction to Session 4

This session focuses on the behavioural aspect of the Cognitive Behavioural Therapy approach which the SMART Programme uses.

This session will enable you to identify which type of behaviours you tend to exhibit – Type A (stress-inducing) or Type B (non stress-inducing). This will show you where you need to make changes.

You will also be provided with information and worksheets enabling you to examine the areas of social support; procrastination; time management; assertiveness; and physical health, so that you can again identify areas where you need to make changes. Some strategies will also be provided.

Finally, so that you can continue to benefit from everything you have learned in the SMART Programme, you will be shown how to create your own personal Stress Management Action Plan. You can refer to this over and over again and amend and update it as your circumstances change over time.

The session and Programme ends with a new relaxation technique – the Progressive Muscle Group Relaxation Exercise.

Go through the next few pages, read the information given and complete the worksheets and the blank Stress Management Action Plan.

CHAPTER NINE

SMART Programme – Session 4 - Overview

Name of Technique/ Content/Activity	Purpose
Type A and Type B Behaviours	Behavioural: You will complete a questionnaire enabling you to recognise Type A and Type B behaviours in yourself. Type A behaviours are stress-inducing. This will enable you to consider making necessary changes, where required.
Using Social Support	Behavioural: You will be able to think of the social support you currently use and identify how this can be improved, if necessary.
Procrastination	Behavioural: You will be able to identify your procrastination behaviours.
Time Management	Behavioural: You will be given some tips on how to improve your time management (if required), as poor time management can lead to unnecessary stress.
Assertiveness techniques	Behavioural: You can consider whether you are assertive enough in the workplace and whether this may be adding to your stress levels. Some assertiveness techniques will be outlined.
Improving Your Physical Health	Behavioural: It is necessary to have healthy bodies in order to be able to cope better with daily stressors. Healthy practices such as a healthy balanced diet; drinking adequate amounts of water; taking adequate exercise, rest and relaxation; and moderate alcohol consumption will be discussed. You will be able to think through any changes you might need to make in order to have a healthier body.
Stress Management Action Plan	Cognitive and Behavioural: You are helped to create a personal Stress Management Action Plan to use after going through the SMART Programme. A completed example is provided.
Physical Relaxation Technique – Progressive Muscle Group Relaxation	Behavioural: Instructions for a gradual tensing and relaxing of muscles exercise are provided.

The SMART Programme

Assessing Type A and Type B Behaviours

Use this exercise to determine whether you tend to exhibit Type A or Type B behaviours. Circle one number for each of the statements below which best reflects the way you behave in your everyday life. For example, if you are generally on time for appointments, for the first point you would circle a number between 7 and 11. If you are usually casual about appointments and don't mind arriving late, circle one of the lower numbers between 1 and 5.

Casual about appointments	1 2 3 4 5 6 7 8 9 10 11	Never late
Non-competitive	1 2 3 4 5 6 7 8 9 10 11	Very competitive
Good listener	1 2 3 4 5 6 7 8 9 10 11	Anticipates what others are going to say (nods, attempts to finish for them)
Never feels rushed (even under pressure)	1 2 3 4 5 6 7 8 9 10 11	Always rushed
Can wait patiently	1 2 3 4 5 6 7 8 9 10 11	Impatient while waiting
Takes things one at a time	1 2 3 4 5 6 7 8 9 10 11	Tries to do many things at once, thinks about what will do next
Slow deliberate talker	1 2 3 4 5 6 7 8 9 10 11	Emphatic in speech, fast and forceful
Cares about satisfying him/herself no matter what others think	1 2 3 4 5 6 7 8 9 10 11	Wants good job recognised by others
Slow doing things	1 2 3 4 5 6 7 8 9 10 11	Fast (eating, walking)
Easy-going	1 2 3 4 5 6 7 8 9 10 11	Hard driving (pushing yourself and others)
Expresses feelings	1 2 3 4 5 6 7 8 9 10 11	Hides feelings
Many outside interests	1 2 3 4 5 6 7 8 9 10 11	Few interests outside work/home
Unambitious	1 2 3 4 5 6 7 8 9 10 11	Ambitious
Casual	1 2 3 4 5 6 7 8 9 10 11	Eager to get things done

Add up all the numbers circled and plot your total below.

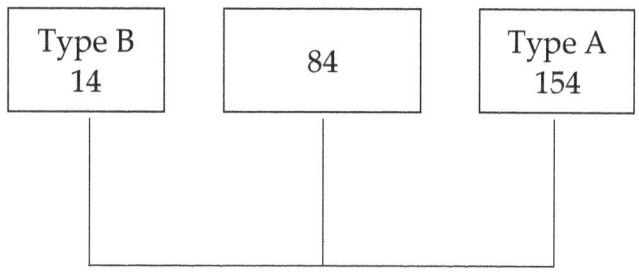

(Footnote: 18)

Most people have a score near 84, generally plus or minus 20. If you scored over 84, you tend towards Type A behaviours and it is easier for you to become stressed. Only the Type A behaviours that actually trigger a stress response in you (e.g. impatience, anger, frustration) need to be modified, as, for example, there are some Type A behaviours such as wanting a good job recognised by others, which are not stress-inducing for some people.

If you scored below 84, then you tend towards Type B behaviours.

You can modify unhelpful, stress-inducing Type A behaviours using the techniques taught in this SMART Programme.

Social Support for Work Problems

Research has indicated that having social support is an important buffer against stress. Think of a situation at work that has caused you a great deal of personal stress. Who did you feel able to talk to about the problem and how helpful did you find them?

Here is a list of people, some of whom you may have spoken to. Think about each one and give them a personal rating between 0 and 5, where 0 is "no support received" and 5 is "a lot of helpful support received".

Person Providing Support	Your Rating
Husband/Wife/ Partner	0 1 2 3 4 5
Mother	0 1 2 3 4 5
Father	0 1 2 3 4 5
Sister	0 1 2 3 4 5
Brother	0 1 2 3 4 5
Other relative	0 1 2 3 4 5
Close friend	0 1 2 3 4 5
Casual friend	0 1 2 3 4 5
Manager	0 1 2 3 4 5
Work colleague	0 1 2 3 4 5
Subordinate	0 1 2 3 4 5
Doctor/Clergy/Therapist/Coach	0 1 2 3 4 5

Examine your ratings. Are there any gaps in your social support network? Is there anyone who you could talk to more or is there anyone who you could add to or take away from the list?

Think about making any necessary changes.

(Footnote: 19)

Social Support for Work Problems (Continued)

Discussing your work problems with someone else should not be seen as a sign of weakness. It may be more helpful to discuss them with someone who can understand your work context or who is task focused; who is confidential; and who may be able to make helpful suggestions. This will help reduce your stress levels.

CHAPTER NINE

Do You Procrastinate?

Think back to the last time you had an important project to complete, papers to mark or a presentation to give. Did you waste any time doing any of the items listed below? Tick the behaviours you performed.

	Cleaning and tidying your desk
	Dusting or tidying your room or computer screen
	Cleaning the kitchen floor
	Washing the windows
	Cutting the grass
	Weeding the garden
	Cleaning the car
	Talking to distant relatives
	Deleting unwanted emails
	Responding to unimportant emails
	Tidying up computer folders
	Surfing the internet
	Playing computer games
	Spending an inordinate amount of time making a priority list
	Spending days preparing for the work by obtaining yet more background information
	Tidying the filing system
	Doing the unimportant jobs in the in-tray
	Answering unnecessary telephone calls
	Consuming more drinks, food or cigarettes than usual
	Whinging to colleagues about the amount of work you have
	Blaming your boss or others
	Telling others that you work best at the eleventh hour (or even later!)

(Footnote: 20)

Procrastination wastes valuable time, which increases stress levels when the job still has to be done but now within a much shorter time-frame.

If you recognise that you tend to procrastinate when under pressure, you can start to do something about it. For example you can identify any unhelpful thoughts you are having and use the strategies and techniques provided by the SMART Programme to stop these. For example, one strategy you could use is the Self-Motivation Imagery and challenges to thinking errors are provided in the tables in Session 2 entitled "Challenging the 15 Thinking Errors".

Time Management Tips

Good time management is one way to control or overcome a lot of your work stress. Here are some tips.

- Make a 'To Do' list at the beginning of the week. Prioritise items in order of importance and deadlines. Refer to your list regularly during the week and revise it as necessary.
- Don't spend too much time on planning, to avoid wasting time.
- When planning, make allowances for unforeseen things.
- Complete one job at a time, to avoid making mistakes.
- Avoid procrastinating. This temporarily relieves stress but a big pay-back comes later. Challenge the unhelpful beliefs or thinking errors that lie beneath this behaviour.
- Be realistic about how much work you and your colleagues can take on at any one time.
- Plan ahead for meetings and itemise points you wish to discuss.
- Think things through before saying yes to the requests of others. If the requested task or project is time-consuming, ask yourself whether you really need to agree to it. Use assertiveness skills and say no when necessary and if possible.
- Try to prioritise incoming mail (postal or electronic), so that you deal with the essential ones first. If you run out of time, the less important mail can be dealt with later.
- Plan the telephone calls you need to make, so that you group them together. Have a list of people you need to call with the things you need to discuss. Keep to the point and avoid being unnecessarily chatty.

Being Assertive

As noted above, one method for conquering stress is good time management. However, it can be difficult to manage your time well without being assertive.

What does being assertive involve? It involves being able to - complain in an appropriate manner; give constructive feedback to others when necessary; defend yourself; ask for what you want; and stand up for yourself. Being assertive can help you avoid the negative experiences of misunderstandings, being taken advantage of and passiveness.

In the following exercise, you will be able to identify the type of behaviour you tend to exhibit, by the section which has the most ticks – aggressive, non-assertive (passive) and assertive.

To reduce your stress levels you will need to reduce the aggressive and passive behaviours and increase the assertive ones. This is because being aggressive tends to lead to conflict and hard feelings, whilst being passive can lead to depression and low self-esteem because you will be feeling walked on and powerless.

Some people may exhibit aggressive behaviour whilst using passive language (a passive-aggressive combination). This is also unhelpful, as although it avoids direct conflict it can be perceived as manipulative, sceptical and spiteful and result in negative behaviour towards you, which can also be stress-inducing.

Complete the worksheet which follows.

CHAPTER NINE

Being Assertive - What Behaviour Do You Tend To Exhibit?

There are 3 types of behaviour that people tend to exhibit: aggressive, non-assertive (passive) and assertive. Tick the ones that you recognise in yourself.

	Aggressive Behaviour
	Finger pointing
	Leaning forward
	Sharp, sarcastic or firm voice
	Fist(s) thumping
	Loud voice/shouting
	Violating of others' rights
	Dominating demeanour
Aggressive Phrases/Words Used	
	You'd better…
	It's your fault!
	You're joking!
	You ought/must/should…
	Don't be stupid!
Non-assertive/Passive Behaviour	
	Shrugging
	Hunched shoulders
	Whining, quiet or giggly voice
	Hand wringing
	Shifting of body weight
	Stepping backward
	Downcast eyes
Non-assertive/Passive Phrases/Words Used	
	Maybe
	Perhaps
	Just
	Only
	I wonder if you could…
	I'm hopeless/useless
	I can't
	Never mind
	It's not important
	I mean
	Well, uh

Being Assertive - What Behaviour Do You Tend To Exhibit? (Continued)

Tick the ones that you recognise in yourself.

Assertive Behaviour	
	Relaxed demeanour
	Lack of hostility
	Smiling when pleased
	No fidgeting/slouching
	Collaborative approach
	Good eye contact
Assertive Phrases/Words Used	
	Cooperative: Let's, we could…
	Open questions: What do you think/want? How do you feel?
	'I' statements: I think, I want, I fear, I feel…

As noted above, the type of behaviour you tend to exhibit to others is indicated by the section in which you have the most ticks.

(Footnote: 21)

I will next set out some assertiveness techniques which you can try out, as relevant to your situation. It is important to note that using assertiveness skills is inadvisable at times, such as when they could result in violence towards you or in you being targeted for dismissal by your boss. It is best to weigh up the situation carefully and if in doubt, use an alternative course of action.

Chapter Nine

Some Assertiveness Techniques

Workable Compromise

Offer the person(s) a compromise, as long as your self-worth or self-respect is not being challenged.

Example:

Your manager: "We are getting desperately behind. Can you come in on Saturday morning and finish the paperwork?"

You: "I've agreed to take my daughter horse-riding tomorrow morning and I'm not prepared to let her down. However, I can start work earlier next Monday and do my best to get the work finished. Is that OK?"

Negative Enquiry

Instead of receiving just global, negative feedback, negative enquiry encourages the other person to provide specific information about your behaviour in a more constructive manner.

Example:

Relative: "You are a totally hopeless parent!"

You: "Can you share with me in what way I am hopeless?"

Broken Record

This involves stating your viewpoint in a relaxed manner while ignoring irrelevant logic or arguments, manipulative traps and/or baiting.

Example:

Student: "You are being really unfair. Why should my results suffer just because my project came in late?"

Tutor: "Unfortunately, the regulations state that a project has to be submitted on the due date, otherwise marks are taken off."

Student: "You've never liked me from the start of the course. I bet you let others off."

Tutor: "The regulations apply to everybody. Marks are taken off if a project is submitted late."

Fogging

By simply acknowledging your mistakes, this skill helps when others are using 'put-downs' or manipulative criticism. This helps you to maintain your self-respect.

Example:

Manager: "Late again! You're letting the office down."

You: "Three months ago I was late when the train broke down, and unfortunately it happened again today."

The 3-Step Model of Assertion

This technique is especially useful when you are under pressure to comply with others' demands.

Step 1: Actively listen to what the other person is saying and demonstrate to them that you have heard and understood what they have said.

Step 2: Say what you think and feel. (A good linking word to use here, between Steps 1 and 2 is 'however'.)

Step 3: Say what you want to happen. (A good linking word to use here, between Steps 2 and 3 is 'and'.)

Example:

Step 1: "It would be nice to go out this evening."
Step 2: "However, I need to prepare for my work tomorrow."
Step 3: "And so I think I'll stay in on this occasion."

If thinking errors (e.g. fear of upsetting others, or having a strong desire for others to like you) and low self-esteem, are preventing you from using assertiveness skills, use the remedial thinking skills provided in the SMART Programme to challenge them. For example, you could use "Challenging the 15 Thinking Errors"; the concept of self-acceptance; or the Stress Thought Record. You can also enlist support from others.

(Footnote: 22)

CHAPTER NINE

Improving Your Physical Health Can Help You Manage and Reduce Your Stress Levels

Key Healthy Practices

- ✓ Taking regular exercise (try to integrate some exercise into your everyday routine). Be careful not to overdo it!
- ✓ Eating plenty of fruit and vegetables.
- ✓ Drinking alcohol, tea and coffee (caffeine intake) in moderation.
- ✓ Drinking adequate amounts of water (on average around 8 glasses per day).
- ✓ Reducing your intake of foods high in saturated fats and trans-fats.
- ✓ Stopping smoking.
- ✓ Controlling your weight – remembering the equation "Body weight is increased when energy intake exceeds energy used." (Palmer & Cooper, 2007, p. 124)
- ✓ Getting adequate rest and relaxation. Rest and relaxation includes firstly getting enough sleep.

Relaxation activities can include:

- ✓ A long warm bath
- ✓ Yoga
- ✓ Breathing techniques
- ✓ Muscle relaxing techniques
- ✓ Massage
- ✓ Going to the spa
- ✓ Listening to your favourite music or to relaxing music
- ✓ Reading a good book
- ✓ Prayer

Avoid Consuming Bad Fats

Consuming <u>saturated fats</u> can lead to restricted and finally blocked arteries, because the fat sticks to the walls of the arteries. This increases blood pressure and may eventually lead to a heart attack. Products containing saturated fats include lard, cheese, butter and the fatty sections of beef, pork and lamb. So it is probably best to eat some of these types of food (e.g. cheese and butter), in moderation and possibly avoid others (such as the fatty sections of the meats).

Trans-fats are a partially hydrogenated vegetable fat used in baked, fried and fast foods which can lead to heart, arterial and other diseases. This is because they cause an increase in the levels of sticky low-density lipoproteins (often referred to as the 'bad' LDL cholesterol) and reduce the healthy high-density lipoproteins (often referred to as the 'good' HDL cholesterol). The bad LDL cholesterol blocks arteries whilst the good HDL cholesterol travels through the bloodstream removing the harmful bad cholesterol from where it doesn't belong. High HDL levels reduce the risk for heart disease but low levels increase the risk.

So it is important to reduce or avoid the intake of foods which increase levels of the bad LDL cholesterol and increase the intake of foods with the good HDL cholesterol. Foods containing trans-fats are therefore best avoided wherever possible.

Increase Your Intake of Good Fats

Polyunsaturated fats are good fats. They benefit the body in various ways including helping to build cell membranes, increasing the good HDL cholesterol levels and assisting in preventing blood clots from forming. They are found in oily fish such as sardines and pilchards. They are also found in vegetable oils such as safflower, sunflower and soya oils.

Mono-unsaturated fats are a liquid fat found in plant-based foods. They are also good fats which increase levels of the good HDL cholesterol and therefore may protect against heart disease. Mono-unsaturated fats are found in canola oil, olives and olive oil, seeds, nuts and avocados. Some mono-unsaturated fat is also found in palm oil. Some research has shown that olive oil may be one of the key elements responsible for the low rate of heart disease among Mediterranean people. It is best to buy extra virgin olive oil wherever possible.

Plant Sterols

Plant sterols lower bad LDL cholesterol levels. These are found in fruit, vegetables, beans, vegetable oils and nuts. They are also available in some yogurts, margarine spreads and drinks. An intake of 2 to 3 grammes of plant sterols per day is recommended to help lower bad cholesterol levels.

Foods to reduce your intake of are:

- Whole milk, cream and yogurt (except for low-fat natural yogurt).

- Meat products such as pork scratchings, meat with fatty portions, pâtés, burgers and sausages (contain unhealthy fats).

- Fried foods (contain saturated fats and trans-fats)

- Tinned fruit in syrup.

- Full-fat cheeses, such as stilton or cheddar.

- Sweetened breakfast cereals, white bread and biscuits.

- ✗ Mayonnaise and salad dressings that are oily and low in mono-unsaturates or polyunsaturates.

- ✗ Salt or foods with a high salt content. First consult your doctor, if you have low blood pressure.

- ✗ Food with a high sugar content, such as sweets, some fizzy drinks and some sweetened fruit juices.

Preferred foods are:

- ✓ Skimmed or semi-skimmed milk.

- ✓ High-fibre foods that assist digestion - including oats, brown rice, wholegrain bread, beans, bran and wholegrain cereals and pasta.

- ✓ Lean meat, poultry or fish. Oily fish are especially healthy (e.g. sardines, pilchards, trout and salmon) but to avoid ingesting too much mercury, eating them no more than 2 to 3 times per week is probably best.

- ✓ Fruit such as bananas, grapes, apples oranges or fruit in natural juices.

- ✓ Cottage cheese, low-fat cheese, or alternatives made with sunflower oil or soya beans.

- ✓ Steamed, grilled or poached food.

- ✓ Mayonnaise alternatives or salad dressings that are low in fat or high in polyunsaturates (e.g. vegetable oils such as sunflower oil) or mono-unsaturates (e.g. olive oil and avocado).

- ✓ Margarines labelled 'high in polyunsaturates' in place of lard or butter.

Sample Stress Management Action Plan

Examine the sample Stress Management Action Plan below and then create your own one using the blank Stress Management Action Plan provided. It may be beneficial if you set a time to check on your progress, e.g. in a month's time. You may then decide to create an amended Plan, so a spare blank Stress Management Action Plan is supplied.

Action to be taken by: Charmaine	Date: 7 March

1. Psychological

<u>Thinking Skills</u>

Stop blowing things out of proportion! Keep events in perspective. Things can be a nuisance but they are rarely catastrophes!

Stop holding on to rigid, demanding 'musts' and 'shoulds'. This will reduce the pressure upon me, my family and staff.

Remember that I am not my behaviour! If I fail at some task, it does not mean that I'm a total failure.

<u>Imagery Skills</u>

If life gets on top of me, use Time Projection Imagery to remind myself that in a few months' time the situation won't seem so bad.

2. Behavioural

<u>Social Support</u>

Make an effort to develop more friendships at work. Have a few more non-work related chats with people. This needn't take up much extra time. I'll start taking tea breaks and chat then.

Start regularly going out to the cinema again with my partner. Make sure we go out with friends at least once a month.

<u>Assertiveness</u>

Practise saying no. Start thinking of the consequences of taking on additional work before answering positively to my colleagues' requests.

Make a big effort to reduce my complaining to my partner and colleagues and stop blaming others so often.

<u>Time Management</u>

Avoid procrastinating! Remind myself that my boss only wants a good job done and not 120 percent. I create real burdens out of tasks due to my thinking errors.

Sample Stress Management Action Plan
(Continued)

Action to be taken by: Charmaine   Date: 7 March
3. Physical Health   <u>Exercise</u>   I'll incorporate exercise into my daily routine: at least three days a week I'll take a walk at lunchtime; at least once a day I'll use the stairs at work and not the lift; I'll take up Squash again and play at weekends.   <u>Nutrition</u>   I'll eat red meat once a fortnight only. I'll attempt to eat oily fish twice a week.   If I fancy a snack, I'll eat some seeds, nuts or fruit.   I'll give coconut milk a go for 2 weeks. If I get used to the taste then I'll continue. I'll drink less coffee and tea and have more herbal teas instead.   <u>Relaxation</u>   Before bedtime I'll spend 10 minutes using the Relaxation Imagery.   At work I'll 'make' the opportunity to use the Relaxation Imagery just before I go home to help me switch off and leave my work stresses where they belong – at work.

(Footnote: 23)

THE SMART PROGRAMME

Stress Management Action Plan

Action to be taken by:	Date:

1. Psychological

2. Behavioural

3. Physical Health

(Footnote: 24)

CHAPTER NINE

Stress Management Action Plan

Action to be taken by:	Date:
1. Psychological	
2. Behavioural	
3. Physical Health	

(Footnote: 24)

Progressive Muscle Group Relaxation

This relaxation technique helps your body to relax. Whole muscle groups are tensed at the same time and then relaxed. Tensing your muscles before releasing them, helps you to recognise what it feels like when your muscles are relaxed. Repeat each procedure at least once, tensing each muscle group from 5 to 7 seconds and then relaxing from 15 to 30 seconds. Remember to pay attention to the contrast between the feelings of tension and relaxation.

Note: When releasing your muscles, do it instantly and let them become suddenly limp, otherwise you may be keeping tension in them.

Instructions

Sit or lie comfortably in a quiet room where you won't be disturbed. You may want to loosen your clothing and remove your shoes. Begin to relax as you take a few slow, deep breaths – in through your nose and out through your mouth. Relax the rest of your body as you tense each muscle group.

1. Curl both fists, tightening biceps and forearms (Charles Atlas pose). Relax.

2. Stretch your arms forward. Hold. Then stretch your hands with fingers straight and wide apart. Hold. Relax.

3. Gently roll your head around on your neck clockwise in a complete circle, then reverse. Relax.

4. Wrinkle up the muscles of your face like a walnut: forehead wrinkled, eyes squinted, mouth opened, and shoulders hunched. Relax.

5. Gently round/hunch your shoulders forward, gently stretching your back forwards. Hold. Relax.

6. Gently arch your shoulders back as you take a deep breath into your chest. Hold. Relax. Take a deep breath, pushing out your stomach. Hold. Relax.

7. Straighten your legs and gently point your toes back toward your face, tightening your shins. Hold. Relax. Straighten your legs and gently curl your toes (forward), simultaneously gently tightening your calves, thighs, and bottom. Relax.

8. Allow your whole body to remain totally relaxed for several minutes.

Note: It is important to do some tensing gently, as indicated, to prevent muscle cramping or spinal damage.

Although you may start by learning to do this relaxation technique in a quiet place, with regular practise, you will be able to do a shortened version of it at any time during the day, when you detect that you are tense.

(Footnote: 25)

Chapter Nine

Homework from Session 4

1. Review all the information you have identified about yourself from this session's activities.

2. From your analysis at point 1 above, pinpoint all the specific areas you need to improve. Make a list for future reference. It may be worth prioritising items in terms of which are more important for you to achieve first. You can tick them off as you achieve them, over the coming weeks and/or months. However, at this moment in time, <u>start with the one which will have an important impact on your life but which is relatively easy to achieve</u>. Achieving this will keep you motivated.

3. Examine your Stress Management Action Plan. Choose to carry out at least one thing in the Plan in the coming week. It may or may not be the same activity chosen at point 2 above.

4. Practise the Progressive Muscle Group Relaxation exercise.

5. Keep your SMART Programme Book, with its completed questionnaires, worksheets and Stress Management Action Plan, in a prominent place, so that you can refer to it as and when required.

6. If you are feeling like procrastinating, don't! Use the Self-Motivation Imagery to help you get started. The benefits will be a happier, less stressful life!

Part Three
General Information

Footnotes

1. From Palmer & Cooper, 2007, p. 41. (Published with permission).
2. From Palmer & Cooper, 2007, pp. 31-34. (Published with permission).
3. Adapted from Palmer & Cooper, 2007, pp. 130-132. (Published with permission).
4. Adapted from Stress Management for the Individual Teacher, by Mills, 1995.
5. From Palmer & Cooper, 2007, pp. 42-43. (Published with permission).
6. From Palmer & Cooper, 2007, p. 48. (Published with permission).
7. Adapted from Palmer & Cooper, 2007, p. 61. (Published with permission).
8. Adapted from Palmer & Cooper, 2007, pp. 63-64. (Published with permission).
9. Adapted from Davis, Eshelman & McKay, 2008, pp. 50-51, 63-64.
10. From Palmer & Cooper, 2007, pp. 68-69. (Published with permission).
11. Adapted from Palmer & Cooper, 2007, p. 70. (Published with permission).
12. From Palmer & Cooper, 2007, pp. 72-73. (Published with permission).
13. From Palmer & Cooper, 2007, pp. 73-74. (Published with permission).
14. From Palmer & Cooper, 2007, p. 82. (Published with permission).
15. From Palmer & Cooper, 2007, p. 84. (Published with permission).
16. From Palmer & Cooper, 2007, p. 85. (Published with permission).
17. From Palmer & Cooper, 2007, p. 86. (Published with permission).
18. From Palmer & Cooper, 2007, pp. 89-91. (Published with permission).
19. Adapted from Palmer & Cooper, 2007, pp. 93-94. (Published with permission).
20. From Palmer & Cooper, 2007, pp. 100-101. (Published with permission).
21. From Palmer & Cooper, 2007, pp. 95-96. (Published with permission).
22. From Palmer & Cooper, 2007, pp. 98-100. (Published with permission).
23. Adapted from Palmer & Cooper, 2007, pp. 152-153. (Published with permission).
24. From Palmer & Cooper, 2007, pp. 154. (Published with permission).
25. Adapted from Davis, Eshelman & McKay, 2008, p. 45-46.

List of References

- Austin, V., Shah, S. & Muncer, S. (2005). Teacher stress and coping strategies used to reduce stress. *Occupational Therapy International,* 12(2), 63-80.

- Bachkirova, T. (2005). Teacher stress and personal values: An exploratory study. *School Psychology International,* 26, 340-352.

- Beck, A.T. & Greenberg, R.L. (1974). *Coping with Depression.* New York: Institute for Rational Living.

- Betoret, F. (2006). Stressors, self-efficacy, coping resources, and burnout among secondary school teachers in Spain. *Educational Psychology,* 26(4), 519-539.

- Bibou-Nakou, I., Stogiannidou, A. & Kiosseoglou, G. (1999). The relation between teacher burnout and teachers' attributions and practices regarding school behaviour problems. *School Psychology International,* 20, 209–217.

- Boyes, C. (2008). *Need to Know? Cognitive Behavioural Therapy. Think better. Be happier.* London: Collins.

- Browers, A. & Tomic, W. (2000). A longitudinal study of teacher burnout and perceived self-efficacy in classroom management. *Teaching and Teacher Education,* 16, 239–253.

- Brown, M., Ralph, S. & Brember, I. (2002). Change-linked work-related stress in British teachers. *Research in Education,* 67, 1-12.

- Butler, A. C., Chapman, J. E., Forman, E. M. & Beck, A. T. (2006). The empirical status of cognitive-behavioral therapy: A review of meta-analyses. *Clinical Psychology Review,* 26, 17-31.

- Chorney, L.A. (1998). Self-defeating beliefs and stress in teachers. *Dissertation Abstracts International,* 58, 2820.

- Curwen, B., Palmer, S. & Ruddell, P. (2000). *Brief Cognitive Behaviour Therapy.* London: Sage.

- Davis, M., Eshelman, E.R. & McKay, M. (2008). *The Relaxation & Stress Reduction Work Book. Sixth Edition.* Canada: New Harbinger

- Dewe, P. J. (1985). Coping with work stress: An investigation of teachers' action. *Research in Education,* 33, 27-40.

- Friedman, I.A. (2000). Burnout in teachers: shattered dreams of impeccable professional performance. *Journal of Clinical Psychology*, 56, 595–606.

- Grimley, B. (2001) 'Simply the stressed!' *The Occupational Psychologist*, 43, 8-12.

- Health and Safety Executive (HSE). (2001). *Tackling Work-Related Stress: A managers' guide to improving and maintaining employee health and well-being*. Suffolk: HSE

- Howard, S. & Johnson, B. (2004). Resilient Teachers: Resisting stress and burnout. *Social Psychology of Education*, 7, 399-420.

- Jarvis, M. (2002). Teacher Stress: A critical review of recent findings and suggestions for future research directions. *Stress News*, 14 (1). Retrieved March 28, 2008, from http://www.enhanceeducation.co.nz/?p=44 and http://www.teachersupport.org/news/218?n=scot

- Jepson, E. & Forrest, S. (2006). Individual contributory factors in teacher stress: The role of achievement striving and occupational commitment. *British Journal of Educational Psychology*, 76(1), 183-197.

- Johnson, S., Cooper, C., Cartwright, S., Donald, I., Taylor, P. & Millet, C. (2005). The experience of work-related stress across occupations. *Journal of Managerial Psychology*, 20, 178-187.

- Klassen, R. (2010). Teacher stress: The mediating role of collective efficacy beliefs. *The Journal of Educational Research*, 103, 342-350.

- Kyriacou, C. (2001). Teacher Stress: Directions for future research. *Educational Review*, 53 (1), 27–35.

- Kyriacou, C. & Sutcliffe, J. (1978). A model of teacher stress, *Educational Studies*, 4, 1-6.

- Lambert, R., McCarthy, C., O'Donnell, M. & Wang, C. (2009). Measuring elementary teacher stress and coping in the classroom: Validity evidence for the classroom appraisal or resources and demands. *Psychology in the Schools*, 46(10), 973-988.

- Lazarus, R.S. & Folkman, R. (1984). *Stress, appraisal, and coping*. New York: Springer.

- McCarthy, C., Lambert, R., O'Donnell, M. & Melendres, L. (2009). The relation of elementary teachers' experience, stress, and coping resources to burnout symptoms. *The Elementary School Journal*, 109(3), 282-300.

- McGrath, B. & Huntington, A. (2007). The health and wellbeing of adults working in early childhood education. *Australian Journal of Early Childhood*, 32(3), 33-38.

- Mills, S.H. (1995). *Stress Management for the Individual Teacher: Self-study Modules for Teachers and Lecturers*. Lancaster: Framework Press.

List of References

- National Institute for Health and Clinical Excellence (NICE). 2004. *Self-harm. The short-term physical and psychological management and secondary prevention of self-harm in primary and secondary care*. London: National Institute for Health and Clinical Excellence.

- Palmer, S. & Cooper, C. (2007). *How to deal with stress*. London: Kogan Page.

- Pithers, R.T. & Soden, R. (1998). Scottish and Australian teacher stress and strain: a comparative study. *British Journal of Educational Psychology*, 68, 269–279.

- Punch, K. F. & Tuettmann, E. (1990). Correlates of psychological distress among secondary teachers. *British Educational Research Journal*, 16, 369-382.

- Richardson, K. M. & Rothstein, H. R. (2008). Effects of occupational stress management intervention programs: A meta-analysis. *Journal of Occupational Health Psychology*, 13, 69-93.

- Roger, D. & Hudson, C. (1995). The role of emotion control and emotional rumination in stress management training. *International Journal of Stress Management*, 2, 119–132.

- Schwarzer, R. & Hallum, S. (2008). Perceived teacher self-efficacy as a predictor of job stress and burnout: Mediation analyses. *Applied Psychology: An International Review*, 57, 152-171.

- Skaalvik, E.M. & Skaalvik, S. (2007). Dimensions of teacher self-efficacy and relations with strain factors, perceived collective teacher efficacy, and teacher burnout. *Journal of Educational Psychology*, 99(3), 611-625.

- Stallard, P. (2002). *Think good-feel good: A Cognitive Behaviour Therapy workbook for children and young people*. Chichester, UK: Wiley.

- van der Klink, J.J.L., Blonk, R.W.B., Schene, A.H. & van Dijk, F.J.H. (2001). The benefits of interventions for work-related stress. *American Journal of Public Health*, 91, 270-276.

Useful Organisations and Websites

- ACAS (Advisory, Conciliation and Arbitration Service) – Provides information on stress, employee and employer rights in the workplace. You can visit their website at: www.acas.org.uk

- BABCP (British Association for Behavioural and Cognitive Psychotherapies) – Provides a list of accredited Cognitive-Behavioural and Rational-Emotive Therapists. These approaches focus on an individual's unhelpful thoughts and behaviours, which is like the approach used by the SMART Programme. You can visit their website at: www.babcp.com/Default.aspx

- Centre for Stress Management & Centre for Coaching – Provides stress counselling, training and coaching services. Uses a CBT approach. You can visit their websites at: www.managingstress.com and www.centreforcoaching.com

- HSE (Health and Safety Executive) - They have a stress home page at: www.hse.gov.uk/stress/standards/index.htm

- International Stress Management Association – Provides information about stress management and accredits stress trainers. You can visit their website at: www.isma.org.uk

- NASUWT – The National Association of Schoolmasters Union of Women Teachers has information regarding stress and how to get support, on their website at: www.nasuwt.org.uk/MemberSupport/MemberGroups.Stress.index.htm

- NUT – The National Union of Teachers has a document entitled "Tackling Teacher Stress" on their website. It can currently be accessed at: www.teachers.org.uk/node/12562

- Teacher Line – Provides 24 hour advice and counselling for UK teachers at: www.teacherline.org.uk and on Tel: 08000 562 561 (England) or 08000 855 5088 (Wales).

- AMHF (The American Mental Health Foundation) – Promotes scientific research and seminars in the field of mental health and related areas. Their website address is: http://americanmentalhealthfoundation.org. You can put "stress" in their search engine to access various articles on stress.

www.ingramcontent.com/pod-product-compliance
Lightning Source LLC
Chambersburg PA
CBHW080924170426
43201CB00016B/2259